Human Sexuality

A Catholic Perspective for Education and Lifelong Learning

UNITED STATES CATHOLIC CONFERENCE

United States Catholic Conference

In accordance with its planning document approved by the general membership of the United States Catholic Conference, the USCC Committee on Education in the Summer of 1988 assumed responsibility for revising *Education in Human Sexuality for Christians*. Given more recent church documents and taking into account pertinent suggestions relating to the earlier guidelines, the Committee determined to prepare an entirely new document to present to the United States Catholic Conference. This document, *Human Sexuality: A Catholic Perspective for Education and Lifelong Learning*, is addressed primarily to diocesan leaders in their service to parents, parishes, and other church-related institutions as they design and implement programs of formal instruction in human sexuality. The final text was approved by the general membership of the United States Catholic Conference on November 21, 1990, and is authorized for publication as a document of the United States Catholic Conference by the undersigned.

Monsignor Robert N. Lynch
General Secretary
NCCB/USCC

December 12, 1990

ISBN 1-55586-405-8

Sexuality is a fundamental component of personality, one of its modes of being, of manifestations, of communicating with others, of feeling, of expressing and of living human love. Therefore it is an integral part of the development of the personality and of its educative process (Congregation for Catholic Education, *Educational Guidance in Human Love* [1983], no. 4).

****

Today, perhaps more than ever before, it is important to recognize that learning is a lifelong experience. Rapid, radical changes in contemporary society demand well-planned, continuing efforts to assimilate new data, new insights, new modes of thinking and acting. This is necessary for adults to function efficiently, but, more important, to achieve full realization of their potential as persons whose destiny includes but also transcends this life (National Conference of Catholic Bishops, *To Teach as Jesus Did* [1972], no. 43).

****

With the help of advances in psychology and in the art and science of teaching, children and young people should be assisted in the harmonious development of their physical, moral and intellectual endowments. Surmounting hardships with a gallant and steady heart, they should be helped to acquire gradually a more mature sense of responsibility toward ennobling their own lives through constant effort, and toward pursuing authentic freedom. As they advance in years, they should be given positive and prudent sexual education (Second Vatican Council, *Declaration on Christian Education* [1965], no. 1).

****

Education in sexuality includes all dimensions of the topic: moral, spiritual, psychological, emotional, and physical. Its goal is training in chastity in accord with the teaching of Christ and the Church, to be lived in a wholesome manner in marriage, the single state, the priesthood, and religious life. Sexuality is an important element of the human personality, an integral part of one's overall consciousness. It is both a central aspect of one's self-understanding (i.e., as male or female) and a crucial factor in one's relationship with others (National Conference of Catholic Bishops, *Sharing the Light of Faith: National Catechetical Directory for Catholics of the United States* [1977], no. 191).

Contents

Introduction

In 1978, the United States Catholic Conference (USCC) appointed a National Committee for Human Sexuality Education. Its members were commissioned to draft a set of instructional guidelines for "a positive and prudent sexual education" in a Catholic context.[1] In 1981, the committee produced a document that was adopted by the USCC Department of Education and published as *Education in Human Sexuality for Christians: Guidelines for Discussion and Planning*.[2]

Since that time, John Paul II and various Vatican congregations have issued a number of pertinent documents related to the area of human sexuality, the family, and education.[3] In 1983, the Congregation for Catholic Education, under the direction of William Cardinal Baum, published *Educational Guidance in Human Love*, subtitled "Outlines for Sex Education." Noting "the cultural and social differences existing in different countries," the Congregation for Catholic Education recommended that their 1983 guidelines "should be adapted by the respective Episcopates to the pastoral necessities of each local Church."[4]

It is commendable that numerous local bishops or statewide Catholic conferences have undertaken to draft sexuality education guidelines focused on the specific needs of a given diocese or

---

1. Cf. Vatican Council II, *Declaration on Christian Education* (October 28, 1965), no. 1.
2. National Committee on Human Sexuality Education/Department of Education, USCC, *Education in Human Sexuality for Christians: Guidelines for Discussion and Planning* (Washington, D.C.: USCC Office for Publishing and Promotion Services, 1981).
3. John Paul II, *Familiaris Consortio* (*On the Family*), Apostolic Exhortation (December 15, 1981); Holy See, *Charter of the Rights of the Family* (October 22, 1983); Congregation for Catholic Education, *Educational Guidance in Human Love: Outlines for Sex Education* (November 1, 1983); Congregation for the Doctrine of the Faith, *Letter to the Bishops of the Catholic Church On the Pastoral Care of Homosexual Persons* (October 1, 1986); Congregation for the Doctrine of the Faith, *Instruction on Respect for Human Life in Its Origin and On the Dignity of Procreation: Replies to Certain Questions of the Day* (February 22, 1987); John Paul II, *Mulieris Dignitatem* (*On the Dignity and Vocation of Women*), Apostolic Letter (August 15, 1988); Congregation for Catholic Education, *The Religious Dimension of Education in a Catholic School* (April 7, 1988). In addition to these official church documents, three collections of the texts of John Paul II's general audiences and conferences also offer valuable insight into human sexuality: John Paul II, *Original Unity of Man and Woman: Catechesis on the Book of Genesis*, General Audiences of September 5, 1979 to April 2, 1980 (Boston: Daughters of St. Paul, 1981); John Paul II, *Blessed Are the Pure of Heart: Catechesis on the Sermon on the Mount and Writings of St. Paul* (Boston: Daughters of St. Paul, 1983); John Paul II, *Reflections on "Humanae Vitae": Conjugal Morality and Spirituality* (Boston: Daughters of St. Paul, 1984).
4. *Educational Guidance in Human Love*, no. 3.

region.[5] Still, as an episcopal conference of bishops, representing the dioceses throughout the United States, we believe it is our responsibility to offer a broader, more national vision, reflecting for the Catholic people of the United States the rich tradition and teaching of the universal Church in the area of human sexuality. Therefore, in the summer of 1988, we formed a new Task Force to revise *Education in Human Sexuality for Christians* in light of more recent church documents, taking into account pertinent suggestions and criticisms of the earlier guidelines.

This second Task Force was composed of twenty-four professional persons, representing the episcopacy, parents, and the fields of catechetics, religious education, human sciences, medicine, mental health, family life, moral theology, and bioethics. They worked diligently over the subsequent two years to produce a revised document, intended for adoption as policy by the National Conference of Catholic Bishops. During the process, the Task Force decided that a mere revision of the previous volume would be less advisable than an entirely new document. The former document focused more on the education of children, with a detailed outline of curriculum objectives and strategies. This document is a foundational one, focusing on the human values, scriptural roots, Christian moral principles, and Catholic theology that underlie curricular policy making. While recognizing that the physical and social sciences contribute valuable insights into our understanding of the human person, we have chosen to develop this document primarily according to scriptural values and church teachings.

We hope that this presentation will foster a greater appreciation of and respect for the precious gift of human sexuality. In this effort, we find ourselves particularly indebted to our present Holy Father, John Paul II, whose concern for the dignity of the human person and for the beauty of human sexuality is reflected in numerous papal pronouncements and pastoral statements.[6]

To whom are we addressing this document? Primarily, we are offering it to guide our diocesan leaders in their service to parents, parishes, and other church-related institutions as they design and implement programs of formal instruction in human sexuality from a Catholic perspective. We echo a strong element of the Catholic educational tradition in affirming the fundamental right

---

5. For helpful resources issued by local bishops or state Catholic conferences see the *Bibliography* at the end of this foundational document.
6. See note no. 3 above for the pertinent documents of John Paul II concerning human sexuality.

and responsibility of parents for the proper nurturing and instruction of their children. "Since they have conferred life on their children, parents have the original, primary and inalienable right to educate them; hence they must be acknowledged as the first and foremost educators of their children."[7] Parents and the family comprise the first and most important matrix for sharing faith, forming attitudes, fostering values, teaching principles, and imparting information.

Others, however, play vital auxiliary roles in the process by which children and adolescents come to understand their sexuality and its expression. Here, we seek a delicate balance between seeing the proper education of our Catholic young people as primarily and ultimately the responsibility of one's parents or legal guardians and a sense that other interested parties—one's wider societal and ecclesial communities—share a familial concern for the welfare of each citizen, each child of God entrusted to us. Among these wider influences are schools, religious education, the media, society at large, and the Church (at the parish, diocesan, national, and universal levels).

In fulfilling its pastoral and educational ministries, the Church recognizes its own serious responsibility to supplement and enhance the education in sexuality, which begins in the home.[8] This is achieved in multiple ways. Through adult enrichment programs, local church communities can offer to adults, whether single or married, parents or not, assistance in their own growth in understanding human sexuality. To those engaged couples approaching a lifelong commitment in marriage, the local Church owes a sensitive and thorough preparation, a vision of Christian marriage in all its facets.

Focusing on parents in particular, the Church can offer guidance in the religious principles involved in the art of raising children. Professional religious educators can help develop catechetical tools for home-based sexuality education, especially of the very young. In cooperation with parents, parochial schools and religious education programs can provide formal instruction programs in human sexuality, geared to the age level and maturity of the children involved. Finally, Catholic church leaders and profes-

---

7. *Charter of the Rights of the Family*, art. 5. See also parallel statements of parental rights in *Declaration on Christian Education*, no. 3; *Decree on the Apostolate of the Laity* (November 18, 1965), no. 11; *Familiaris Consortio*, nos. 36-37;

8. Cf. *Declaration on Christian Education*, no. 3; Vatican II, *Pastoral Constitution on the Church in the Modern World* (December 7, 1965), no. 52; *Educational Guidance in Human Love*, no. 64.

sional educators also can assist parents and public schools in designing programs for sexuality education that are values-based.

In particular, in the United States, we are sensitive to the ethnic and cultural diversity of our people as well as to the variety of family models. Families come in many forms and configurations today: nuclear, extended, single or multiple generations, two-parent, single-parent, single-earner, dual-earner, and dual-career.[9] At the same time, a child's family environment is influenced by a variety of other socioeconomic factors: the rising cost of living; the increased desire for consumer goods; the greater number of single-parent, separated, or blended families; the increased rate of divorce in recent decades.[10] We strongly encourage family life specialists and sexuality educators from the various special communities within this country to translate the universal values, principles, and norms we propose here into sexuality education programs and materials that will meet the specific needs of individuals, families, and communities.

While this document is written particularly for diocesan leaders, its focus is on the collaborative efforts of these professionals to assist parents or guardians in presenting a view of human sexuality that is Catholic and values-based as well as adapted to their own family situation. Whether such assistance focuses on sexuality education in the home or in a more formal setting or in some combination of the two, the full participation of parents at every step in the process—planning, implementation, and evaluation—will foster the "family perspective" so essential to inculcating values and a deep-rooted respect for one's own sexuality and that of others.[11] We hope, therefore, that many parents and parents' organizations will find this document helpful in their efforts not only in the home but also in assisting community leaders to develop fuller, values-based, Christian-influenced sexuality education programs.

Finally, one's growth in understanding human sexuality does not end with puberty or marriage or some subsequent threshold in life. The Catholic Church teaches that human life is to be valued

---

9. See Ad Hoc Committee on Marriage and Family Life, NCCB, *A Family Perspective in Church and Society: A Manual for All Pastoral Leaders* (Washington, D.C.: USCC Office for Publishing and Promotion Services, 1988), p. 28. This volume is a helpful resource for sociological data about marriage and family in the United States.
10. See Bishops' Committee for Pastoral Research and Practices, NCCB, *Faithful to Each Other Forever: A Catholic Handbook of Pastoral Help for Marriage Preparation* (Washington, D.C.: USCC Office for Publishing and Promotion Services, 1989), pp. 10-12. This is a thorough and pastorally helpful 154-page resource book.
11. *A Family Perspective in Church and Society* [see footnote no. 9 above] offers a helpful model for viewing education within the family relational network as distinct from solely imparting information to individuals. See also, *Educational Guidance in Human Love*, no. 72.

and safeguarded from the moment of conception. The need to relate sexual feelings with the Christian call to love and to be loved is a lifelong task for each of us. Education in sexuality is a continual process, an invitation for each of us to grow and develop as morally mature sexual beings, whatever our age or calling in life. We encourage ongoing formation in human sexuality not only for children and adolescents but also for all people, particularly during major transitions in life (e.g., puberty, moving away from home, engagement/marriage, parenthood, middle age, retirement, divorce or widowhood, ordination, religious vows, aging, serious illness).

Therefore, in the widest sense, this document is addressed to all Catholic people of our many dioceses across the United States, to other Christians, to Jews with whom we share so much, and to all people of good will who may find solidarity with us in this search for a healthy and wholesome approach to living our human sexuality. Throughout this document, we strive to be affirming and positive about the gift that is our human sexuality, while also being mindful of the genuine responsibility associated with living and directing this gift wisely and lovingly.

The document that follows is divided into five chapters and an appendix:

Chapter 1 presents an overview of human sexuality from the Judaeo-Christian perspective, drawn mostly from the Book of Genesis and reflections on the incarnation of Jesus. Sexuality is seen both as a wonderful gift and an awesome responsibility.

Chapter 2 offers a portrait of what it means to be psychologically whole and spiritually holy. Sexuality is an area in which each person must seek to synthesize bodily feelings with spiritual values.

Chapter 3 surveys some of the Catholic principles, human values, and moral implications of living one's sexuality well.

Chapter 4 focuses on particular groups and specific sexual issues. The joys and difficulties of married life, living as a single person, being homosexual, choosing celibacy, and growing through adolescence are all treated with candor and understanding. This chapter also contains brief explanations of the Church's moral teaching regarding specific sexual topics, including responsible parenthood, nonmarital sex, homosexuality, and masturbation.

Chapter 5 outlines some of the parameters and processes recommended for educational efforts in human sexuality. A partnership of family, school, religious education, Church, and society is presented as the ideal.

The *Appendix* offers more specific guidelines for education in human sexuality. These guidelines outline basic principles from this document and make particular recommendations for educating about human sexuality at five stages of human development.

It behooves all of us to approach the mystery of incarnation and our sexuality with a degree of humility. We are aware of the depth and complexity of the topic. This document is offered as our contribution to the ongoing discussion about what it means to be mature sexual persons—physically, psychologically, socially, and spiritually whole.

Chapter 1
Human Sexuality
Wonderful Gift and
Awesome Responsibility

The Book of Genesis reveals that at the very dawn of creation, humanity was created in the image and likeness of God, male and female they were created. And God saw all creation, including sexually differentiated human beings, as "very good."[1] Thus, our gender, our sexual identity as male or female persons, is an intimate part of the original and divine plan of creation. The mystery of what it means to be human—incarnate, embodied, and therefore sexual—is bound up in the mystery and purpose of God, who is the author of all life, and love itself.

So, from the outset, we want to be clear that we believe human sexuality is a gift. We approach the topic of human sexuality with a deep and abiding sense of appreciation, wonder, and respect. We are dealing with a divine gift, a primal dimension of each person, a mysterious blend of spirit and body, which shares in God's own creative love and life.

Christian theology has long reflected on the revelation of God as a communion of persons, the Trinity. God's inner life is a life of radical sharing and communication among the Father, Son, and Holy Spirit. It is in, through, and out of that mysterious love within God that all life and love come. Created in God's own image, we find inscribed in our hearts one core universal vocation, that is, to love and to be loved.[2] Love is our origin; love is our constant calling on earth; and love will be our fulfillment in heaven.[3]

John Paul II speaks of each person "as an incarnate spirit, that is, a soul which expresses itself in a body and a body informed by

---

1. Genesis 1:26-27 (*New American Bible* trans.). An overview of a theology of Creation is found in, National Conference of Catholic Bishops, *Sharing the Light of Faith: National Catechetical Directory for Catholics of the United States* (Washington, D.C.: USCC Office for Publishing and Promotion Services, 1979), no. 85.

2. Cf. *Pastoral Constitution on the Church in the Modern World*, no. 12; *Familiaris Consortio*, no. 11.

3. Cf. "Wedding Preface III," *The Roman Missal*.

an immortal spirit."[4] Acknowledging that love is "the fundamental and innate vocation of every human being" the pope goes on to say that "love includes the human body, and the body is made a sharer in spiritual love."[5] We are created not as angels or pure spirits but as human beings, embodied and sexual. We make incarnate God's own goodness, love, and vitality in our frail human efforts to love.

In Genesis, chapter two, the second version of the story of creation, God says, "It is not good for the man (Adam) to be alone. I will make a suitable partner for him." God then fashioned a woman to be Adam's equal partner, out of his "rib." When at last he sees Eve, Adam is ecstatic and exclaims, "This one, at last, is bone of my bones and flesh of my flesh." And the inspired author concludes, "That is why a man leaves his father and mother and clings to his wife, and the two of them become one body."[6] From this passage, and its usage across the Christian tradition, we see that sexuality is intimately related to our vocation to love, our natural yearning for committed relationships.

The Christian tradition has also understood this passage as illustrating a natural mutuality and equality that exist between man and woman. "The sexes are complementary: similar and dissimilar at the same time; not identical, the same, though, in dignity of person; they are peers so that they may mutually understand each other, diverse in their reciprocal completion."[7] Both man and woman are *persons*—equal yet distinct. "The gift of sexuality involves the whole person because it permeates all facets of the human personality: the physical, the psycho-emotional, the intellectual, the spiritual and ethical, and the social."[8]

"Sexuality" and "Sex": Related, but Distinct Realities

Sexuality is a relational power, not merely a capacity for performing specific acts.[9] The Vatican Congregation for Catholic Education speaks of *sexuality* as "a fundamental component of personality, one of its modes of being, of manifestation, of com-

---

4. *Familiaris Consortio*, no. 11.
5. Ibid.
6. Genesis 2:23-24.
7. *Educational Guidance in Human Love*, no. 25; See also *Familiaris Consortio*, no. 22.
8. The Bishops of the Dioceses of New Jersey, *A Joint Pastoral Statement on Education in Human Sexuality* (1980), no. 2.
9. See Cardinal Joseph Bernadin, *Sexuality and Church Teaching* (September 29, 1980). Text prepared for delivery to the bishops gathered at the 1980 International Synod on the Family.

municating with others, of feeling, of expressing and of living human love."[10] Sexuality prompts each of us from within, calling us to personal as well as spiritual growth and drawing us out from self to interpersonal bonds and commitments with others, both women and men. It includes the qualities of sensitivity, understanding, intimacy, openness to others, compassion, and mutual support.[11]

Sexuality is a dimension of one's restless heart, which continually yearns for interpersonal communion, glimpsed and experienced to varying degrees in this life, ultimately finding full oneness only in God, here and hereafter. "In the fullest and richest sense, the gift of sexuality is both the physical and psychological grounding for the human person's capacity to love. . . . It is a gift shared by all persons, regardless of their state in life."[12]

In our own *National Catechetical Directory*, promulgated as guidelines for religious education in the United States, we proposed, "Sexuality is an important element of the human personality, an integral part of one's overall consciousness. It is both a central aspect of one's self-understanding (i.e., as male or female) and a crucial factor in one's relationships with others."[13] Therefore, throughout this document, we distinguish between this broader, more inclusive and relational term *sexuality* and the more restrictive act-specific term *sex:*

> *Sexuality* refers to a fundamental component of personality in and through which we, as male or female, experience our relatedness to self, others, the world, and even God.

> *Sex* refers *either* to the biological aspects of being male or female (i.e., a synonym for one's gender) *or* to the expressions of sexuality, which have physical, emotional, and spiritual dimensions, particularly genital actions resulting in sexual intercourse and/or orgasm.

Since the divine vocation to love is deeply rooted in each person as a "unified totality," and since each cell of the human body bears the female or male genetic imprint, it is proper to speak of sexuality and one's sexual response in a wide variety of interpersonal situations in which genital arousal and response are not pertinent.

---

10. *Educational Guidance in Human Love*, no. 4.
11. See Bishop Francis Mugavero, "Sexuality—God's Gift: A Pastoral Letter," reprinted in *Catholic Mind* (1976): 54.
12. Ibid.
13. *Sharing the Light of Faith*, no. 191.

Accordingly, we ought not to reduce our educational efforts related to sexuality solely to a study of specific acts and their moral implications.

The Incarnation: An Affirmation of Our Humanity

We find in the Paschal Mystery, the story of our redemption in Christ, further affirmation of our material world and our sexual nature. The *incarnation* of God's Word, the divine becoming fully human, adds even greater dignity or divine approbation to our being corporeal, sexual beings. The annunciation, birth, life, death, and resurrection of Jesus Christ serve as a divine affirmation of the goodness and lovableness of humanity. Jesus of Nazareth, as revealed in the gospel stories, was fully embodied, like us in all things but sin. He was single and chaste, but he was not neuter. Jesus was a man of deep feelings, love, and commitment—to God, the Father; to his mother; to his disciples; and, in a particular way, to personal friends like Mary, Martha, Lazarus, Mary Magdalene, Peter, James, and John, "the beloved disciple." Likewise, we who bear the name *Christians* are called to experience and express human love as whole persons—body, mind, and soul.

Precious Gift Implies an Awesome Responsibility

Like all our human powers and freedoms, sexuality, a gift from God, can be channeled for good or ill. Each of us is entrusted by God with the responsibility to guide and direct this gift wisely and lovingly. At best, our sexuality calls us to personal maturity and interpersonal commitments.

> It should not be surprising that the power and pleasure which are part of sexuality will demand of us intelligence, honesty and sacrifice that might test our maturity to the utmost degree. But we do not fear sexuality, we embrace it. What we fear at times is our own inability to think as highly of the gift as does the God who made us sexual beings.[14]

Unfortunately, the story of Adam and Eve does not end at chapter two of Genesis, with blissful mutual happiness in the

---

14. "Sexuality—God's Gift: A Pastoral Letter," in *Catholic Mind*, p. 54.

Garden of Eden. Human insecurity, pride, and selfishness soon set in and with them come the effects of sin—relational hardships, painful human labor, and a tarnishing of the divine image. Salvation history is filled not only with stories of sexual fidelity and commitment but also with tales of sexual misuse or abuse. The adulterous affair of David and Bathsheba illustrates well how sexuality, when combined with other passions and motives, can lead to suspicion and jealousy rather than loving intimacy, to personal destruction rather than new life.[15]

The reality of *original sin* remains the inevitable counterpoint to all our efforts to promote a healthy, holistic, and Christian approach to life, including human sexuality. While we are called to incarnate the image of God in the way we live and love, the gift of human sexuality also can be abused, sometimes intentionally, sometimes through immaturity or ignorance. Given how important sexuality is to one's self-concept and interpersonal attractions, such errors in judgment frequently have a profound impact for ill on one's psyche, human commitments, and relationship with God.[16]

It is a fundamental belief of the Christian tradition that, left to our own efforts and without grace, we are unable to overcome sinful temptations and to attain our personal and eternal destiny. Temptations to subvert our human desires, including sexual ones, into purely selfish aims or to manipulate others in human relationships have become deeply rooted in our hearts and in human history. And many succumb to these temptations.

The Scriptures, the Nicene Creed, and our Christian faith assure us that only through the incarnation and redemption of Jesus Christ can we achieve true holiness, able to overcome temptation, whether sexual or otherwise. It is only by cooperating in the ongoing redemptive work of the risen Christ that we can confidently call all people to live out the image of God imprinted within.

Reflections on the Sexual Revolution

Beginning in the mid-1950s and continuing to the present, the people of the United States have been involved in what many have called a "sexual revolution." Believing that societal sexual values and mores were the product of an overly restrictive, somewhat anti-body bias, proponents of this revolution advocated a greater appreciation of the beauty, pleasure, and goodness both of being

---

15. See 2 Samuel 11—12.
16. Cf. *Educational Guidance in Human Love,* no. 44; *Sharing the Light of Faith,* no. 98.

sexual and of expressing oneself sexually. It was suggested that being more open and candid about sexual feelings and desires might liberate people from what some felt were inordinate fears and unfounded taboos.

Genital activity, including sexual intercourse, reserved in the Christian tradition exclusively for marriage, has been proposed by some as reasonable and appropriate in a wide variety of less committed, sometimes even purely recreational and uncommitted settings. Nonmarital sexual intercourse seems to have become culturally acceptable, perhaps even the statistical norm. The related use of contraceptives to prevent pregnancies in marital and nonmarital situations has become more common, particularly with the advancing medical technology related to "the pill" and prophylactic devices. Homosexual activity, ranging from committed cohabitation to casual genital sex, has become more socially acceptable, at least in certain sections of the country.

This movement toward greater sexual license, while not neatly cause and effect, has had an impact on the rise in marital infidelities, separations and divorce, nonmarital sex and cohabitation, teen pregnancies, sexually transmitted diseases, and greater exploitation via pornography and seems related to the steady increase in the number of abortions of convenience. The Puritanism, chauvinism, sexual repression, and negative emphasis vis-à-vis almost everything sexual that tended to mark an earlier cultural era has been replaced by comparable or even greater excesses in the opposite direction.

While victims of the former sexual repression might develop negative self-esteem and inordinate guilt about sexual inclinations themselves, victims of the newer sexual revolution mentality tend to become easily involved in promiscuous or recreational sex. Our underlying concern is that any holistic or Christian discussion of sexual morality must be grounded in a more personal appreciation of human dignity, of the value of life itself, and of the depth, complexity, and responsibility attached to human interpersonal relationships, including their sexual dimension.

The Advent of Sexuality Education Programs

Over the past two to three decades, sexuality education has been introduced into a number of school systems or church-related programs, in an attempt to meet the challenge of living in a sexually permissive and pluralistic society. Some of these programs focused almost exclusively on the biology of reproduction and contraception. Often the prevention of teen pregnancies or sexually transmitted diseases was their sole or primary aim. Others attempted a more values-oriented approach, blending basic anatomical information with a focus on the mature development of the whole person.

In curriculum planning for parochial schools and religious education programs, there has been greater awareness of the need for a faith-rooted, values-based presentation of human sexuality. While intramural disagreements have arisen as to what values ought to be highlighted and which programs best serve the task, there is a consensus that if formal instruction in human sexuality is to be offered, it ought to be taught from a values-based perspective, in which values are based on faith. The difficulty in the more pluralistic public-school setting has been to determine which values are widely accepted as beneficial for the entire community. Nevertheless, sexuality education even in public schools ought to foster family values, respect the dignity of the human person, stress personal responsibility, promote wholesome relationships, and recognize the demands of parenting. We urge parents and educators alike to reflect on those basic moral laws inscribed in the human heart and conscience and to derive from them the principles in which our children's moral lives are to be formed.

In Summary

In this chapter, three underlying Christian convictions have emerged:

First, human sexuality, a core dimension of the human need to love and to be loved, is a gift from God, which commands appreciation, wonder, and respect. "Sexuality is an enrichment of the whole person—body, emotions and soul—and manifests its innermost meaning in leading the person to the gift of self in love."[17]

Second, being sexual, like being intelligent or athletic or gifted in any other way, is a two-edged experience. We can respectfully

---

17. *Familiaris Consortio,* no. 37.

13

direct this gift in a manner reflective of our human dignity and God's gracious design, or we can misuse or even abuse ourselves and others by irresponsible sexual actions.

Third, the incarnation and redemptive life, death, resurrection, and promised return of Jesus Christ make available the inspiration and grace to respond more fully to God's invitation to live a sexually responsible life.

Therefore, it is with hope that we summarize this chapter. With God's abiding love and grace, shared with us in and through the cross and resurrection of Jesus Christ, and now made available to all humanity through the Spirit who dwells in human hearts, and who acts in a special way through the Church and the sacraments, we can now live and love responsibly as male and female. With God's help, we can experience, enjoy, and make wise and loving use of one of God's special gifts, our human sexuality.

Chapter 2
Sexuality and
the Christian Life
A Universal Calling to
Wholeness and Holiness

"In light of the Mystery of Christ, sexuality appears to us as a vocation to realize that love which the Holy Spirit instills in the hearts of the redeemed."[1] Whether one is called to be married, single, ordained, or a vowed religious, love is our origin, our constant calling, and our fulfillment in the kingdom to come.[2] Jesus' proclamation that he has come that we "might have life, and have it to the full"[3] refers both to our more immediate concerns with this life as well as our hope for life eternal.

Each of us is a sexual being, embodied with a gender, influenced by hormones and sexual stimuli, called to channel and direct this dimension of ourselves toward love and life and holiness. Married people experience their sexuality in a variety of ways, including conjugal love and genital intercourse. Infants, children, and adolescents are also sexual persons. So, too, are single adults, divorced and widowed people, and homosexual men and women. Vowed and professed celibates likewise remain sexual beings, for they achieve sexual maturity, in part, because of their commitment to an intense, exclusive relationship to God and God's world in nongenital ways. Since sexuality is a fuller, more pervasive reality within humanity than its genital expressions, dealing creatively with one's own sexuality—gender, sexual feelings, and desires—becomes a fundamental challenge in every person's quest for spiritual integrity and psychological well-being.

---

1. *Educational Guidance in Human Love, no. 30.*
2. Cf. "Wedding Preface III," *The Roman Missal; Familiaris Consortio, no. 11.*
3. John 10:10.

Wholeness and Holiness
A Lifelong Conversion Process

This chapter, therefore, focuses on the universal calling in every human heart to be personally whole and spiritually holy. In this world "all of us seek happiness: life, peace, joy, and a wholeness and wholesomeness of being."[4] These desires for personal and social fulfillment are natural and good. But through the gift of faith and the grace to live faithfully, Christians discern that the desire for earthly well-being is a reflection of an even more profound desire of the human heart, the longing for union with God here and hereafter.

The challenging task of becoming a mature person—physically developed, psychologically integrated, interpersonally responsible, and spiritually holy—is made all the more difficult by the reality of human sinfulness. "The disorder provoked by sin, present and operating in the individual as well as in the culture which characterizes society,"[5] exercises a strong pressure to conceive and live life, including our sexuality, in a manner opposed to the law of Christ. John Paul II echoes the Christian tradition in calling for "a continuous, permanent conversion,"[6] an ongoing transformation of our minds and hearts.

Conversion, as Paul VI defined it so well, is "a profound change of the whole person by which one begins to consider, judge, and arrange one's life according to the holiness and love of God."[7] This concept of a lifelong conversion process, linked as it is to seeing as God sees, has been associated in the Christian tradition with the notion of spirituality. Unfortunately, for some, the very idea of *spirituality* has come to mean some "other-worldly piety," marked by "withdrawal" or "separation" from this world as much as possible. There is truth in the ascetical tradition, in its desire that one not be "possessed" by worldly cares or by one's possessions. Still, that is not the same as withdrawal or isolation in any anti-world sense. We believe that "the spiritual life is, above all, life. It is concerned with ultimate meanings and values, but it is incar-

---

4. National Conference of Catholic Bishops, *To Live in Christ Jesus: A Pastoral Reflection on the Moral Life* (Washington, D.C.: USCC Office for Publishing and Promotion Services, 1976), no. 17.
5. *Educational Guidance in Human Love*, no. 44.
6. *Familiaris Consortio*, no. 9.
7. Paul VI, *Paenitemini* (February 17, 1966), cited in *To Live in Christ Jesus*, no. 14.

nated in human encounters and circumstances."[8]

For Christians, *spirituality* "consists in the living out in experience, throughout the whole course of our lives, of the death-resurrection of Christ that we have been caught up into by baptism."[9] It is the process, whereby a person rejects the tempting but illusory destructive forces that isolate and alienate one from human encounters. That interior movement from alienation to reconciliation, expressed and incarnated in our learning to love—God, our neighbors, ourselves—is at the heart of both Christian faith and psychological good health.[10]

This is not to imply that the search for spiritual wholeness in and of itself offers neat and tidy solutions to one's psychological or interpersonal challenges. Neither the power of prayer nor other spiritual exercises can supplant hard work. Spiritual contemplation and basic human effort "are interdependent elements of one ascending spiral of life in Christ, of being caught up in Christ Jesus."[11]

Those very human virtues and practices that foster personal integration or interpersonal love and commitment serve to translate and symbolize the life of the Spirit. "They contain glimpses of the Lord." In reality God, who is love, is "the transcendent Third" in all human relationships.[12]

True Love Is Greater than Personal Enjoyment

"To love" and "to be loved" are two phrases bantered about much in our vocabulary. The phrase "I love you" is used to express our affection or positive feelings for people as diverse as one's spouse, children, parents, or close friends. At the same time, the word *love* is often mistakenly used to describe our fondness for things, inanimate objects that we use and enjoy solely for our own pleasure and comfort. But, true love is greater than personal enjoyment. "The love required for a close, committed, long-term rela-

---

8. Ad Hoc Committee on Priestly Life and Ministry, NCCB, *Spiritual Renewal of the American Priesthood* (Washington, D.C.: USCC Office for Publishing and Promotion Services, 1972), pp. 2-3. The Task Force on Human Sexuality found this volume, while originally focused on the spirituality of priests, to be helpful for discussing spirituality as it relates to all people.

9. Ibid., p. 3.

10. Cf. *Faithful to Each Other Forever*, pp. 48-53. This section contains in more detail a helpful discussion of the conversion process from alienation to reconciliation.

11. *Spiritual Renewal of the American Priesthood*, p. 5.

12. Cf. ibid., pp. 46-47.

tionship, for the type of intimacy essential in a satisfying friendship or a successful marriage, must, on the other hand, be self-giving or unselfish, as well as steady and sometimes even courageous."[13]

As much as one hopes that love will bring with it enjoyment, pleasure, and some measure of happiness, the Scriptures, particularly the Gospels and writings of St. Paul, remind us that true *love* is patient and kind, not self-seeking. Jesus said that no one has greater love than to lay down one's life for one's friends; and St. Paul reminds us that real love is always ready to excuse, to trust, to hope, and to endure whatever comes.[14] This is not meant to imply that human beings love in a totally selfless way. In caring for and about others, we certainly hope, all things being equal, to be cared for and nurtured in return. But love does not promise that things will always be equal. Love is a "personal decision characterized by commitment, self-sacrifice, and perseverance. It isn't an emotion, and it certainly isn't sexual activity."[15] Yet, our sexuality, as distinct from sexual activity, is indeed one of the innate motivating forces that draw us out of ourselves into loving relationships.

"Autonomy" and "Relatedness" A Delicate Balance

Whether single or married, old or young, each person must find his or her own unique balance between autonomy and relatedness. By *autonomy* we mean "separateness, independence, and being 'other.'" By *relatedness* we mean "bonding, closeness, and being 'one with.'"[16] The quest for a healthy balance between the two, a reasonable degree of independence of thought and action, blended with an ability to trust, to share, and to rely on others, is a difficult and ongoing task. Because our personalities are different, our individual family settings are distinct, and our cultures vary, there is no single measuring rod, no universal synthesis for all people.

Jesus Christ serves as a model who blends the capacity for autonomy with a profound concern for the well-being of others. Still, his own first-century Galilean experience—the balance of desert retreats with wedding feasts and Jewish festivals; his acceptance and rejection by others; his relationships with family and

---

13. *Faithful to Each Other Forever*, p. 30.
14. See John 15:13; 1 Corinthians 13:7.
15. Rev. John Bertolucci, *On Fire with the Spirit* (Ann Arbor, Mich.: 1984), p. 111, cited in *Faithful to Each Other Forever*, p. 30; see also Thomas Aquinas, Summa Theologica, IIa-IIae, Question 27, art. 2.
16. *Faithful to Each Other Forever*, p. 32.

friends—bespeak his unique calling, influenced by his own time, place, history, culture, and temperament. Like Jesus, each of us is called to discern within his or her own life the best balance of autonomy and loving relatedness.[17]

Chastity: A Universal Challenge

Woven through every search for genuine love, for personal maturity, and for interpersonal commitments, is a call to be chaste, sexually responsible, and appropriate for one's particular vocation or state in life. *Chastity* "consists in self-control, in the capacity of guiding the sexual instinct to the service of love and of integrating it in the development of the person."[18] Chastity is often misunderstood as simply a suppression or deliberate inhibition of sexual thoughts, feelings, and actions. However, chastity truly consists in the long-term integration of one's thoughts, feelings, and actions in a way that values, esteems, and respects the dignity of oneself and others. Chastity frees us from the tendency to act in a manipulative or exploitive manner in our relationships and enables us to show true love and kindness always.

It is not easy to be chaste in contemporary American society. A natural curiosity about sex and a sincere desire for intimacy are given greater license by peer pressure and a culture that romanticizes and trivializes all things sexual.[19] A person seeking maturity and balance, someone striving to live Christian love, "practices the virtue of chastity by cultivating modesty in behavior, dress, and speech, resisting lustful desires and temptations, rejecting masturbation, avoiding pornography and indecent entertainment of every kind, and encouraging responsible social and legal policies which accord respect for human sexuality."[20]

In attempting to present the principles of sexual morality to children and adolescents, the Church strives to assist the young to become aware of Catholic teachings without, at the same time, creating excessive feelings of guilt, shame, or discouragement. In the past, too many adolescents have withdrawn from the practice of their faith and disparaged the Church rather than facing their shortcomings and seeking forgiveness, since their exaggerated feelings of guilt seemed, to them, unbearable.

---

17. Cf. *Spiritual Renewal of the American Priesthood*, p. 14.
18. *Educational Guidance in Human Love*, no. 18.
19. Cf. *Faithful to Each Other Forever*, p. 34.
20. *Sharing the Light of Faith*, no. 105.

The authors of *Educational Guidance in Human Love* suggest that in order to move toward maturity in the affective dimensions of sexuality, one needs to learn self-control, "which presupposes such virtues as modesty, temperance, respect for life and others, openness to one's neighbor."[21] Modesty and temperance both involve a sense of balance, an ability to dress and act appropriately in given situations. The old adage "moderation in all things" captures, to some degree, the spirit of these two related virtues or good patterns for living one's vocation responsibly. Underlying and grounding the practice of modesty and temperance is a deep and abiding respect for life, one's own and that of others, as highlighted by the authors of the Vatican document.

In *Faithful to Each Other Forever,* seven virtues were singled out as reflective of the responsible Christian conscience. To a large extent, these echo the virtues just mentioned and serve to summarize the general focus of this chapter. Each of us, in the context of his or her own ongoing conversion, should strive to be open to life, generous and sacrificing (not selfish), trusting, wise, humble, mutual, and church-guided.[22]

The Love of Christ
A Multifaceted Source of Grace

Left to our own devices such discipline would be extremely difficult, in all likelihood too much for us. Fortunately, Christ has not left us orphans in our struggle for wholeness and holiness. His farewell gift of the Spirit offers us abundant aid and insight for the task of living love fruitfully as embodied, sexual persons. The Spirit of God abounds in our world, abiding and working:

in each of us, male and female, created in the image and likeness of God;

in the family, the "domestic church," which is called to be in miniature an image or locus of the Body of Christ;

in the Church, the living Body of Christ in time and space, and in a special way in the Magisterium of pope and bishops, the official teachers of the Church;

21. *Educational Guidance in Human Love,* no. 35.
22. Cf. *Faithful to Each Other Forever,* pp. 40-41.

in the inspired Word of God, revealed in history, yet ever fresh and vital;

in the sacraments, each instituted to give, strengthen, and renew God's life in us throughout our journey;

in communal prayer, wherever two or three gather in Christ's name;

in the lives and stories of Mary, the mother of Jesus, and of the saints, both those who have gone before us marked with the sign of faith and those uncanonized saints who live in our midst even today; and

in the recesses of each human heart, where prayer, conscience formation, and discernment find holy ground.

All vocations in life find their ultimate grounding in the common call to be baptized and to live as temples of God's Spirit. Grafted to the vine who is Christ, each person must seek out his or her specific path to the fullness of the kingdom. Along the way, the Eucharist serves as our bread of life, helping us to face honestly and to conquer all obstacles to holiness.[23] At the same time, the Lord's Supper is the summit and source of unity and life for the whole Christian family, the Church.[24]

In a similar way, the sacrament of reconciliation is a ready and renewing source of personal and interpersonal healing. In speaking a word of compassion to married couples, Paul VI set a tone applicable to people in any vocation: "And if sin should still keep its hold over them, let them not be discouraged, but rather have recourse with humble perseverance to the mercy of God, which is abundantly poured forth in the sacrament of penance."[25] Whatever vocation one is called to live, there will be need for repentance and mutual forgiveness along the way. Frequent recourse to the Church's sacrament of reconciliation serves both as a source of healing grace and as an impetus to incorporate humility, mercy, magnanimity, and an ability to forgive into one's daily life.

---

23. Cf. *Educational Guidance in Human Love,* no. 45; *Familiaris Consortio,* no. 57.
24. See Vatican II, *Constitution on the Sacred Liturgy* (December 4, 1963), no. 10.
25. Paul VI, *Humanae Vitae* (July 25, 1968), no. 25; *Familiaris Consortio,* no. 58; *Educational Guidance in Human Love,* no. 45.

21

A Spiritual Companion
A Friend for the Journey

In recent years, there has been a resurgence of interest in choosing a confessor, a spiritual director, or a spiritual "friend" as a sojourner along the way. While each of these terms connotes a particular focus or expertise, we welcome the practice of sharing faith journeys, of seeking the wise counsel and candor of others as one struggles to discern his or her unique vocation and strives to live it in wholeness and holiness. One's spiritual companion could be a trained spiritual director, perhaps an ordained cleric, for such professionals are often helpful guides in the discernment process. One's spiritual companion might be his or her spouse or closest, dearest friend. Often one's spiritual companion or guide is someone older, wiser, perhaps from a different walk of life, or with a unique angle of vision. This person, one would hope, has done some deep reflection about life, faith, and love. He or she can serve as a confidant, someone to help keep us honest and on course.

Moral Decision Making and Personal Discernment: A Catholic Approach

One might ask, "How do I know if I've chosen correctly? Is this the morally right thing to do? How do I know if I've chosen the right vocation? How do I know if this course of action, this relationship or this chosen life-style is best for me? How do I know if I'm called to be single or married or ordained or a vowed religious?" There are few easy answers. Whether one is facing specific moral decisions or broader vocational questions, the Catholic tradition speaks of *discernment* as that process by which a person uses one's own reasoning ability, the sources of divine revelation (Scripture and tradition), the Church's teaching and guidance, the wise counsel of others, and one's own individual and communal experiences of grace in a sincere effort to choose wisely and well.

Moral decision making is a particular type of discernment process. In order to decide the right course of action, particularly about matters that may be complex or controversial, Catholics must be open to the wisdom of God manifest in all those sources cited earlier in this chapter—one's family, the Church, the Word of God, the sacraments, communal and private prayer, the stories of the saints. At the same time, data from the physical sciences, information from the social sciences, and the insights of human reason can all contribute to one's discovering moral truth.

The bishops gathered at the Second Vatican Council reaffirmed that Christian morality is determined by *objective standards*. "These, based on the nature of the human person and his or her acts,"[26] are not intended to preempt human evaluation and discernment, but neither are they reducible solely to sincere intentions or an evaluation of motives.

The Catholic tradition has generally accepted a tiered or sequential approach to Christian ethics, as reflected in the traditional levels of natural law theory. Certain values and derived norms remain timeless and absolute. At the most basic or objective level are certain principles and values that reflect human nature as imprinted by the design and will of the Creator. The belief that "good is to be sought and evil avoided" is one such fundamental principle.

Similarly, the inherent and abiding worth of such basic values as life, love, and truth are indisputable. Each is a constitutive dimension of human well-being to be preserved and fostered if one is to be a responsible and virtuous person. People of all races, nations, and times have been able to discover and affirm these as true. The Church holds that "there can be no real conflict between the teaching of reason and faith correctly understood."[27] Whether through reasoned reflection or Spirit-inspired revelation, *or both*, humanity can discover, at least in general outline, the meaning of life, the image of God incarnate in the human heart and history.

In some instances, the linkage between a core value and the subsequent positive or negative norm derived from it is so self-evident that the prescription or proscription shares the absoluteness of the value itself. For example, if one accepts that human life is a value, that a certain dignity adheres innately to all living members of the human species, then certain actions, particularly if specified carefully, would in all cases be right or wrong. Thus, the Church holds that the direct killing of the innocent (e.g., abortion, euthanasia, murder, bombing aimed at noncombatants) as well as all directly intended bodily harm to innocent persons (e.g., rape, child or spouse abuse, and torture) are always and everywhere morally wrong.

---

26. *Pastoral Constitution on the Church in the Modern World*, no. 51.
27. *Faithful to Each Other Forever*, p. 27. This concept is drawn from Vatican Council I, *Constitution on Faith and Reason*, DS 3017.

In other instances, the linkage between fundamental values, norms for behavior, and specific case applications, while real, is more difficult to discern. While we agree that one should always do the "loving thing" or the "life-respecting thing," determining what that means in terms of a given case or context may not be so self-evident. For example, when, if ever, is it "loving" or "life-respecting" to cease life-sustaining treatment on a terminally ill patient? While the Church believes there are still objectively right and wrong answers to such moral dilemmas, the process of moving from absolute values to general norms to specific case judgments requires the virtue of *prudence*. Prudence refers to the ability to exercise sound judgment in practical matters.[28] Prudence is one of the four cardinal or hinge virtues of the Christian tradition.

John Paul II notes that this prudential or providential discernment process is accomplished through the "sense of faith," which is a gift given by the Holy Spirit to all the faithful. "The Church, therefore, does not accomplish this discernment only through the pastors, who teach in the name and with the power of Christ, but also through the laity."[29] Particularly, in the area of education in human sexuality, the pope notes that we depend on lay specialists such as physicians, lawyers, psychologists, social workers, and consultants to offer "their contribution of enlightenment, advice, orientation and support."[30]

Still, as the bishops reaffirmed at Vatican II, there is a special teaching role or office within the Church, entrusted to the bishops in communion with the pope. "Endowed with the authority of Christ," it is our responsibility, "by the light of the Holy Spirit," to discern and to teach the faith that is to be believed and put into practice.[31] It is our unique duty, in conjunction with the Holy Father and other bishops of the world, "to ensure that the Church remains in the truth of Christ" and to lead the People of God ever more deeply into that truth through "an even more mature evangelical discernment."[32]

Finally, there is the area of subjective responsibility. The Church has consistently taught that a person of sincere conscience may have perceived and acted on a moral situation in a manner incon-

---

28. See Thomas Aquinas, *Summa Theologica*, IIa-IIae, Questions 47-56; A standard work on the cardinal virtues, including a chapter devoted to prudence, is Josef Pieper, *The Four Cardinal Virtues* (New York: Harcourt, Brace & World, 1954/1965). Translated from the original German.

29. *Familiaris Consortio*, no. 5.

30. Ibid., no. 75.

31. Vatican II, *Dogmatic Constitution on the Church* (November 21, 1964), no. 25.

32. *Familiaris Consortio*, no. 5. See parallels in *Dogmatic Constitution on the Church*, no. 12; Vatican II, *Dogmatic Constitution on Revelation* (November 18, 1965), no. 10.

sistent with the teaching of the Church. Still, provided she or he did so with no intentional malice or desire to do wrong, the Christian tradition has recognized mitigated *subjective* culpability for a decision that *objectively* is wrong and ought not to have been made. Subjective culpability is determined by how diligently one strives to form correctly his or her conscience and how sincerely one follows that conscience.

In light of this distinction between the *objective* and the *subjective*, Catholic parents, bishops, pastors, teachers, and religious educators must defend the objective truth we believe is embodied in our tradition and provide pastoral care for those who fail to understand, dissent, or make sincere mistakes. We must teach with courage and fidelity the Church's doctrines concerning sexuality and sexual morality, calling upon Catholics to accept them. At the same time, we must offer compassion and understanding to those who fail to discern or to live out God's loving will.[33]

Aware that conversion is a gradual process, John Paul II suggests that the image of the Church as "teacher" and "mother" is apt. As teachers, we must never tire of proclaiming objective moral values and norms as we discern them across the centuries. But, like a caring mother or father, we must remain close to those who "find themselves in difficulty"[34] believing or living some important aspect of the moral life.

Educators in human sexuality must develop this same skill. They must be able to convey the Church's teachings regarding sexual morality and the various vocations in life with authority, candor, sound reasoning, fidelity, and a sensitivity to the age and maturity level of their audience. At the same time, effective educators must take the time to listen to questions, concerns, and insights from the learners; to respect their integrity and sincerity; and to facilitate their ongoing search for knowledge and a deeper understanding of truth about the mystery of human sexuality.

In the end, whether choosing one's vocation or making a moral decision that relates to or affects one's vocation, each person is bound to live with and to stand by his or her own discernment or perception of God's will. In either case, "the art of discernment of spirits comes into play. If the content of the experience is in harmony with the gospel data of revelation and tradition and results

---

33. See *Faithful to Each Other Forever*, p. 46. This a helpful treatment of the need for both courage and compassion in marriage and sexuality catechesis.
34. *Familiaris Consortio*, no. 33. See parallels in *Humanae Vitae*, nos. 28-29; National Conference of Catholic Bishops, *Human Life in Our Day* (November 15, 1968); *Sharing the Light of Faith*, no. 190.

in a rekindling of faith, strengthening of hope, and fostering of love, then it probably is an experience of God. A sense of greater integrity, peace, and joy or renewed call to a personal conversion of heart are validating qualities."[35]

Ultimately, each person—whether single or married; whether widowed, divorced, or celibate; whether adult or adolescent—must discern his or her own moral decisions and wider vocational calling. With all the input and support possible, both from individuals and communities, one must still face the future based on decisions made before God in the recesses of one's own heart. As the bishops at Vatican II phrased it, "Conscience is the most secret core and sanctuary of a person. There one is alone with God, whose voice echoes in the depths."[36]

In Summary

This chapter has been about wholeness and holiness, the one Christian call "to love"—God, neighbor, and self. Such a calling involves all facets of one's life. Ideally, each person strives to be physically developed, psychologically integrated, interpersonally responsible, and spiritually holy. This chapter centered on the wider, more universal calling to be loving and chaste, whatever one's vocation is in life.

Given the powerful individual and cultural pull toward self-centeredness and sin, each person must pursue a personal, lifelong journey of conversion by which one tries to "consider, judge and arrange one's life according to the holiness and love of God."[37] Christian spirituality, rightly understood, implies ongoing conversion. The spiritually maturing person experiences again and again, throughout the whole course of one's life, a sharing in the Paschal Mystery of Jesus Christ. Our lives become a reflection of the death and resurrection of Christ each time we die to our own selfishness or excessive drive for autonomy and rise to live blamelessly before God and interdependently with others.

Genuine love does not promise constant enjoyment, pleasure, and happiness. While hoping for a measure of reciprocity, some degree of mutuality in love relationships, a person whose love is true is willing to go the extra mile, to turn the other cheek, to be

---

35. *Spiritual Renewal of the American Priesthood*, p. 44.
36. *Pastoral Constitution on the Church in the Modern World*, no. 16.
37. *Paenitemini*, as cited in *To Live in Christ Jesus*, no. 14.

committed in bad times as well as good.[38] Self-giving and sacrifice, fidelity, courage, patience, kindness, forgiveness, hope, perseverance—these are some of the virtues reflective of true love, whether one is married, single, or celibate. Each person is called to live chastely, sexually responsible in his or her distinct vocation and life-style. Chastity is evident when one practices self-control, modesty, and temperance, all grounded in a deep respect for oneself and others.

On our own, we are destined to fail at times, to fall short in our efforts to love truly and to live chastely. But God's love, poured out in Christ and made available through the Spirit, surpasses all our imaginings. It graces us for the conversion journey. Where sin or self-centeredness abound, God's redemptive grace abounds more. In each of us, in our families and networks of friends, God is present. So also, God's Spirit abides in the Church, in the Word of God and the sacraments, in prayer, and in the lives of saints living and dead. Finally, the Spirit dwells in the recesses of each human heart, where conscience formation and discernment ultimately converge.

To be humanly whole and spiritually holy is a universal and integrating challenge. Each of us is called to be sexually responsible and chaste in whatever vocation we discern. God's grace is sufficient for us, if we are open and responsive to it. The conversion process has begun, but it is not complete in any of us. Confident in God's promise and presence, yet aware of our own frailty and sin, may we be courageous yet compassionate, forthright yet humble along the way. We encourage all members of the Church to draw strength, comfort, and renewed challenge from the Word of God, the Eucharist, and the healing and strengthening power of the sacrament of reconciliation.

---

38. Cf. Matthew 5:38-42; see also, "Rite of Marriage," *The Roman Ritual*.

Chapter 3
The Divine Plan Inscribed in Human Sexuality
A Catholic Perspective

In the previous chapter, we laid the groundwork for a Christian vision of what it means to be a sexual being, holy and whole. Every person is a sexual being, called to be *chaste*, that is, to do what is sexually responsible for one's state in life. In this chapter, we will outline some of the fundamental values that ground a Catholic approach to sexual morality. Certain derivative moral norms follow logically, and these will be presented candidly, though with a sensitivity to those at various stages in the discernment and conversion process. Some of these values and norms are "sex-specific." By that we mean that they derive directly from our belief in the "language" or "nuptial meaning" of the body, the inherent and abiding significance related to gender differentiation and sexual functions.

A Theology of the Body— Meaning Imprinted Within

The story of Adam and Eve (Gn 2—3) serves as a paradigm through which the Church has discerned and refined some basic moral values related to sexual activity. Based on this biblical teaching that man and woman were made for each other, the Catholic tradition affirms that they share a basic mutuality and equality.

> Man and woman constitute two modes of realizing, on the part of the human creature, a determined participation in the Divine Being: they are created in the "image and likeness of God" and they fully accomplish such vocation not only as single persons, but also as couples, which are communities of love.[1]

---

1. *Educational Guidance in Human Love*, no. 26.

29

Drawing on that same passage, the Church states that, generally, "it is not good for the human to be alone." Loneliness, a feeling of needy isolation or estrangement, is one of life's basic and painful experiences. The desire not to be alone, to be loved and to love, to be united with another, physically as well as psychologically and spiritually, is a deep-seated and natural yearning. Seeing in Adam and Eve a model for human intimacy, the Judaeo-Christian tradition upholds that "community of life and love," which we call marriage, as the natural and divinely ordained context for living together and lovemaking.

Likewise, the story of creation, as recounted in the first chapter of Genesis, indicates that marriage and sexual love are also ordained for "the procreation and education of children."[2] Hence, the divine command to "be fruitful and multiply" (Gn 1:28) is coupled with the realization that "it is not good for the human to be alone" (Gn 2:18) to yield a twofold understanding of the meaning of marriage and its rightful status as the proper context for genital sexual activity.

In the Second Vatican Council document *Constitution on the Church in the Modern World*, the bishops together with Paul VI offered a succinct summary of the Church's fundamental teaching on marriage and sexual morality.[3]

> The intimate partnership of married life and love has been established by the Creator and qualified by God's laws. It is rooted in the conjugal covenant of irrevocable consent. Hence, by that human act whereby spouses mutually bestow and accept each other, a relationship arises, which by divine will and in the eyes of society too, is a lasting one. For the good of the spouses and their offspring as well as of society, the existence of this sacred bond no longer depends on human decisions alone.[4]

Thus, marital commitment and fidelity provide the stable environment in which *sexual intercourse*, variously called the "marital act" or an expression of conjugal love, finds its true meaning as *an act of loving union* and *potentially an act of procreation*. The genitally expressed love of married couples can and ought to be fruitful or

---

2. Scripture scholars debate which of the two creation accounts is older. Both are in the inspired text of the Book of Genesis. The Second Vatican Council and the 1983 *Code of Canon Law* conclude that the two values, *unitive* and *procreative*, are of equal importance.
3. See *Pastoral Constitution on the Church in the Modern World*, nos. 47-52. This chapter of the document is entitled "Fostering the Nobility of Marriage and the Family."
4. Ibid., no. 48.

creative in a variety of ways, even when the procreation of children is not possible or advisable at a given time.

Echoing this twofold interpretation of the meaning of genital sex, John Paul II refers to sexual intercourse as "by no means something purely biological," but as an intimate action that expresses in physical terms "total personal self-giving," with a rightful respect for "the demand of responsible fertility."[5] He speaks of the "nuptial meaning of the body," a phrase that states the Catholic conviction that the bodily act of sexual intercourse of itself always bespeaks a depth of interpersonal commitment and an openness to the possibility of procreation appropriate only in marriage.[6]

God, who is love and the author of life, has inscribed in sexual intercourse two meanings that are inseparable: love and life. The gift of the body in sexual intercourse is a real symbol of the giving of the whole person. If the person were to withhold something or reserve the possibility of deciding otherwise in the future, by this very fact he or she would not be giving totally. When a man and woman give themselves to one another in sexual intercourse, becoming "one body" as Scripture says, this love does not end with the couple, but makes them capable of a great and special gift—the gift by which they become cooperators with God in giving life to a new human person.[7]

It is this inherent, natural, divinely ordained linkage of the *unitive* and *procreative* meanings of human sexual intercourse, as discerned in human nature, the Scriptures, and Catholic tradition, that has led us as a church community to the conclusion that only in marriage can genital sexual expressions find their true meaning.[8] Only in the context of a "matrimonial covenant, by which a man and a woman establish between themselves a partnership of the whole of life,"[9] does genital sex serve as an incarnate symbol of human communion, with an openness to the possibility that children may be the fruit of this two-in-one-flesh encounter.

The Church's teaching here is rooted in a profound respect for the dignity and irreplaceability of human persons. When a husband and wife give themselves to one another in sexual intercourse, the act unites two persons who already, by their marital commitment, have made each other irreplaceable in their lives. At

---

5. *Familiaris Consortio*, no. 11.
6. Cf. ibid., no. 37.
7. See *Original Unity of Man and Woman*, pp. 106-112.
8. See *Familiaris Consortio*, no. 11.
9. *Codex Iuris Canonici* (*Code of Canon Law*), 1983 ed., c. 1055.1.

the same time, it unites persons who, by their free choice to marry, have the capacity and responsibility to welcome new human life and to provide for the proper nurturing, faith development, and education of children so conceived.

It is easy to understand why the Church, especially through the parish community, seeks to help people preparing for marriage. Couples contemplating marriage are accepting a "lofty calling."[10] As Paul VI phrased it, "Marriage is not, then, the effect of chance or the product of evolution or unconscious natural forces; it is the wise institution of the Creator to realize in humanity God's design of love."[11] When a woman and man make the decision to marry, they accept the calling to form a "community of love," bound by a commitment that is deeper, more permanent than any civil contract. Their mutual exchange of vows symbolizes and seals a covenant bond, an unbreakable pledge of fidelity. For their own individual and mutual good, for the benefit of offspring, as well as for the stability of society, the existence of this human bond depends on divine support.

The bishops at Vatican II declared that "authentic married love is caught up into divine love and is governed and enriched by Christ's redeeming power and the saving activity of the Church."[12] In the case of professing Christians, a "special sacrament" enriches and ennobles their married love. The man and woman profess to each other solemn vows of love and fidelity, which serve as the outward sign of an interior reality. Thereafter, Christ resides with them in a powerful way so that, enlivened by the Holy Spirit, they may continue to love each other faithfully. They are called to reflect in their life together an image of the "Savior's living presence in the world" and of the abiding love between Christ and the Church.[13]

Marriage Preparation, Reflective of a Tradition

By providing thorough marriage preparation, in which the couple has the opportunity to reflect on the nature of the marriage relationship, the joys as well as the problems of married life, we

---

10. *Pastoral Constitution on the Church in the Modern World*, no. 47.
11. *Humanae Vitae*, no. 8.
12. *Pastoral Constitution on the Church in the Modern World*, no. 48.
13. Cf. *Faithful to Each Other Forever*, pp. 1-2; *Familiaris Consortio*, nos. 12-13.

hope to launch them well into living this lifelong sacrament. Marriage preparation ought not to be seen solely in terms of some weekend retreat or a six-night mini-series immediately preceding the wedding. In 1989, the Bishops' Committee for Pastoral Research and Practices concluded several years of work with the publication of *Faithful to Each Other Forever*. Subtitled "A Catholic Handbook of Pastoral Help for Marriage Preparation," this volume echoes John Paul II's conviction that effective preparation for marriage is "a gradual and continuous process."[14] It includes three main stages—remote, proximate, and immediate formation—together with support throughout the years of married life together.

Any program attempting to teach the meaning of human sexuality from a Catholic perspective would necessarily focus much time and attention on the meaning of the marriage covenant, as an indissoluble or unbreakable union and commitment between a man and a woman. It is there that sexuality finds its full and proper genital expression, embodied in so many ways, some routine, others romantic and pleasurable, but always intimate and special. The Church recognizes sexual union as a special privilege and blessing. Prior to or separated from the marital commitment, sexual intercourse ceases to be an expression of *total* self-giving.

Thus, we affirm the Church's clear teaching that sexual union is legitimate (has its true meaning and moral rectitude) only in the context of marriage.[15] Outside of this "definitive community of life" called marriage, however personally gratifying or well intended, genital sexual intimacy is objectively morally wrong. "However firm the intention of those who practice such premature sexual relations may be, the fact remains that these relations cannot ensure, in sincerity and fidelity, the interpersonal relationship between a man and a woman, nor especially can they protect this relationship from whims and caprices."[16] Relational misunderstandings and breakups, the sense of being used or betrayed, the trauma of unexpected pregnancies, sometimes followed by abortion of the young, constitute some of the real personal harm that can result from sexual intimacy expressed apart from the bonds and fidelity of marriage.

---

14. Cf. *Familiaris Consortio*, no. 66; see also, *Faithful to Each Other Forever*.
15. Cf. Congregation for the Doctrine of the Faith, *Declaration on Certain Questions Concerning Sexual Ethics* (December 29, 1975), no. 7; *Faithful to Each Other Forever*, p. 33; *Familiaris Consortio*, no. 11.
16. *Declaration on Certain Questions Concerning Sexual Ethics*, no. 7.

Personal, Interpersonal, and Procreative Concerns

We realize that this particular teaching, namely, that sexual intercourse is a human good reserved to married couples, may not be well received by some people. It is common in our American culture for couples engaged to be married or couples contemplating formal engagement or even couples who feel close affection and friendship, even if marriage is not likely, to engage in intimate sexual expressions, including sexual intercourse. The romanticism of theatrical, film, or television dramas; the lure of media advertisements building on "love story" themes; the peer pressure to be sexually intimate fairly early in a budding relationship; and the strong personal need or drive for swift and immediate closeness all coalesce to foster what we believe is a premature and misguided focus on sex and genital expressions.

The potential harm does not stop at "sincere" sexual activity by caring, but nonmarried couples. All too often, particularly among teenagers and those inexperienced in human relationships, sexual exploitation preempts any attempt at true love and commitment. As pastors, we see so many situations in which sexual intercourse done casually or primarily for one's own selfish pleasure, whether premaritally or extramaritally, has caused real psychological, social, and spiritual damage.

Social scientists suggest that our current American society is marked by tendencies toward excessive individualism and a preoccupation with self-gratification. So also, the consumerism of our age, with the correlative practice of built-in obsolescence and disposable goods, tends to make permanence, commitments, and fidelity seem "old-fashioned" or even unattainable.[17] The young and inexperienced are particularly vulnerable to manipulation through false pledges of love and fidelity. Their fragile egos and adolescent sense of self make them easy prey to sexual demands couched in the language of romantic love.

Nor is the potential harm limited to psychological and spiritual damage to the individuals involved. The procreative potential of sex means that a third party, a new member of the human family,

---

17. See *Faithful to Each Other Forever*, pp. 13-15. Similar concerns have been written about in the widely read and critiqued volumes: Robert Bellah, Richard Madsen, William Sullivan, Ann Swidler, Steven Tipton, *Habits of the Heart* (Berkeley: University of California Press, 1985); National Conference of Catholic Bishops, *Economic Justice for All: Pastoral Letter on Catholic Social Teaching and the U.S. Economy* (Washington, D.C.: USCC Office for Publishing and Promotion Services, 1986).

can be affected, at least potentially, by every act of intercourse. We join parents, other community leaders, public policy experts, and educators who are concerned about the dramatic rise in unwed teenage pregnancies. Recent statistics indicate that more than half of America's teens have experienced sexual intercourse by the time they are seventeen. More than 1 million teenage girls in this country become pregnant each year. That has resulted in a 200 percent increase in the birth of children to unwed teenage mothers in recent decades. Even with that dramatically increased birthrate, still more than 400,000 teenage girls now have abortions each year.[18] No single approach, whether educational, motivational, or legal, will stem this tide of children bearing or aborting children. Still, we express our concern and our dedication to seeking long-range solutions—for the sake of the persons involved, for the sake of the children conceived, and for the stability of society as a whole.

Likewise, each person has a personal obligation not to risk being infected or infecting others with sexually transmitted diseases (STD). These can cause serious mental and physical harm, frequently including infertility and sometimes even death. The flesh-and-blood stories of the lives and tragic deaths of so many men, women, and infected children compel us to speak out for personal and sexual fidelity and against the spread of such human misery through irresponsible sexual choices.

Sexuality Education: Information within the Context of Formation

While we wish to prevent young women and their sex partners from having to face the trauma of conception and pregnancy before they are married, and while we seek the prevention and eradication of all sexually transmitted diseases, we do not accept the rationale that underlies sexuality education programs that offer only the "quick fix"—an easy solution. Programs that facilitate easy access to contraceptive devices or that are focused primarily on preventing unwanted pregnancies or sexually transmitted diseases are shortsighted and foster irresponsible behavior.[19]

We are convinced that easy access to condoms and contraceptive pills and devices and the promotion of a false sense of confidence

---

18. Cf. *Faithful to Each Other Forever*, p. 26; see also, William J. Bennett, then U.S. Secretary of Education, "Sex and the Education of Our Children," Speech Delivered to the National School Boards Association, Washington, D.C., as reprinted in *America* (February 14, 1987): 120-125.

19. Cf. *Educational Guidance in Human Love*, no. 19; *Familiaris Consortio*, no. 37.

associated with the "safe sex" slogan are not the answer to these crises.[20] Commitment, fidelity, responsibility—all within the context of marriage—will better serve to ensure that children conceived will be children accepted and cared for and that sexually related diseases will be isolated and not spread further. A sexuality education campaign aimed at fostering loving commitments and social responsibility not only will serve the goals of preventing teen pregnancies and sexually transmitted diseases, but also will serve the persons involved and the society at large by fostering greater societal and family stability.

We recommend programs in sexuality education that offer clear and accurate factual information about sexual gender identity, puberty/adolescence, and human reproduction, appropriately adapted to the age and maturity level of the learner. But such *information* ought to be communicated within the context of *formation,* guided by the values and responsibilities of the whole person, physical, psychological, social, and spiritual. In a values-based sexuality education program, the presentation of a set of basic Judaeo-Christian or societally endorsed positive values and corresponding cautions or prohibitions is essential.

In addition to providing accurate information, sexuality education programs, to be adequate, must do more than teach *about* values and beliefs. They must promote and encourage behaviors reflective of these values. Obviously, care must be taken to respect the requirements of freedom. Even so, the impact of strong models, constructive peer pressure, and appropriate sanctions should not be underestimated.

Such programs ought to include values related to self-respect and self-esteem as well as those pertaining to the human dignity of all persons, social responsibility, and a sensitivity to the vulnerability inherent for each person in experiencing and expressing one's sexual self. Particularly in the areas of family relationships and sexuality education, pastoral sensitivity to the various cultures in the Church and society needs to be exercised. For Christians, scriptural values related to walking in the footsteps of Christ and living in the Spirit supplement and deepen our understanding of basic societal goods. For Catholics, the Scriptures, church tradition and teaching, the sacraments, the leaders, and all the members of the Body of Christ serve continually as God-given sources of insight and grace.

---

20. See National Conference of Catholic Bishops, *Statement on School-based Clinics* (Washington, D.C.: USCC Office for Publishing and Promotion Services, 1987).

In Summary

In this chapter, we have presented the basic framework for a theology of human sexuality from the Catholic perspective. Grounded in the belief that the gift of sexuality has been entrusted to us to be directed wisely and lovingly, we proceeded to discern within the book of Genesis the outline or imprint of the Creator in our very nature and bodies. Created male and female by God's design, man and woman are naturally drawn to union with one another, physically, psychologically, socially, and spiritually.

The story of creation recorded in Genesis 2—3 speaks eloquently of human loneliness, of one person's yearning for an equal partner, a helpmate for life. This deeply experienced need for "covenant" or complete union with a single beloved partner has come to be known as the *unitive* dimension of human relationships and sexual attraction, written, as it were, in the very heart or nature of each woman and man. It finds its ecclesial and societal expression in that "community of life," which we call marriage.

At the same time, the account of creation in the first chapter of Genesis speaks of the *procreative* dimension of sexual union, the call to "be fruitful, multiply, fill the earth, and subdue it." The desire of married couples to procreate, to generate new life, both in terms of offspring and in terms of other mutually creative endeavors, is a natural, divinely ordained instinct.

Across the centuries, the Church has developed a theology of marriage and sexual morality grounded in these two aspects: the *unitive* and the *procreative* dimensions related to gender differentiation and sexual activity.[21] From these values discerned in nature and the Scriptures, the Church has derived two norms related to sexual behavior, which were highlighted in this chapter. First, that genital sexual union is morally permissible—has its true meaning and moral rectitude—only in the context of marriage. Second, outside of the context of covenant commitment (i.e., marriage), genital sexual intimacy, however well intended, is not an expression of *total* self-giving. Objectively speaking, it is morally wrong, and subjectively, one may be guilty of serious sin.[22]

---

21. See *Codex Iuris Canonici*, c. 1051.1. This canon articulates in succinct form the theology promulgated by the bishops in union with the pope gathered in ecumenical council: "The Matrimonial covenant, by which a man and a woman establish between themselves a partnership of the whole of life, is by its nature ordered toward the good of the spouses and the procreation and education of offspring; this covenant between baptized persons has been raised by Christ the Lord to the dignity of a sacrament" (cf. *Pastoral Constitution on the Church in the Modern World*, nos. 47-52).
22. Cf. *Declaration on Certain Questions Concerning Sexual Ethics*, no. 7; *Familiaris Consortio*, no. 11.

We conclude the chapter by restating our belief that all programs in human sexuality ought to include accurate and candid "information" appropriate to the age and maturity of the learners involved, all within the context of "formation" based on abiding human values, principles, and norms. In addition, sexuality programs under church auspices must be informed by the Scriptures, Christian tradition, the sacraments, and the authentic teaching office of the Catholic Church.

Chapter 4
Special Groups
and Sexual Issues
Moral Discernment
and Pastoral Care

In this chapter, we want to speak candidly concerning the lifestyle or vocation of various persons or groups and about some of the sexual issues that face them directly. This presentation of Catholic sexual morality is intended for adults, rather than as a primer for elementary schoolchildren. It is intended to assist diocesan leaders and religious educators in responding to those who ask *what* the Church really teaches about particular sexual issues and *why*. The content presented here also should be incorporated into sexuality education as age, maturity, and needs dictate.

Conjugal Love and Responsible Parenthood

The bishops gathered at the Second Vatican Council presented carefully written observations on Christian marriage and on conjugal love, a synthesis of the Christian tradition that has served as the basis for subsequent teachings by both Paul VI and John Paul II.[1] An overview of this theology comprised the major portion of chapter three of this present document. In summary:

> The intimate partnership of married life and love has been established by the Creator and qualified by His laws. It is rooted in the conjugal covenant of irrevocable personal consent. Hence, by that human act whereby spouses mutually bestow and accept each other, a relationship arises which by divine will and in the eyes of society

---

1. Cf. *Pastoral Constitution on the Church in the Modern World*, no. 47-52; *Humanae Vitae*; *Familiaris Consortio*.

too is a lasting one. For the good of the spouses and their offspring as well as of society, the existence of this sacred bond no longer depends on human decisions alone.[2]

The bishops went on to describe two innate, abiding, and inseparable meanings, which God has inscribed in human hearts, in the nature of human sexuality and in the "communion of life" called marriage:

The Unitive Meaning

This love [between husband and wife] is an eminently human one since it is directed from one person to another through an affection of the will. It involves the good of the whole person. . . .

This love is uniquely expressed and perfected through the marital act. The actions within marriage by which the couple are united intimately and chastely are noble and worthy ones. Expressed in a manner which is truly human, these actions signify and promote the mutual self-giving by which spouses enrich each other with a joyful and thankful will.[3]

The Procreative Meaning

By their very nature, the institution of matrimony itself and conjugal love are ordained for the procreation and education of children, and find in them their ultimate crown. . . .

Children are really the supreme gift of marriage and contribute very substantially to the welfare of their parents. . . .

Hence, while not making the other purposes of matrimony of less account, the true practice of conjugal love, and the whole meaning of family life which results from it, have this aim: that the couple be ready with stout hearts to cooperate with the love of the Creator and the Savior, who through them will enlarge and enrich His own family day by day.[4]

Perceiving that this final statement might imply that marriages of older individuals or of persons unable to bear children are somehow inferior or second class, the bishops affirmed that "marriage persists as a whole manner and communion of life, and maintains its value and indissolubility, even when offspring are lacking—despite, rather often, the very intense desire of the couple."[5]

In 1968, Paul VI issued an encyclical letter, *Humanae Vitae*, in which he echoed this theology of marriage and conjugal love.

---

2. *Pastoral Constitution on the Church in the Modern World,* no. 48.

3. Ibid., no. 49.

4. Ibid., nos. 48, 50.

5. Ibid., no. 50.

Seeing marriage as more than "the product of evolution or unconscious natural forces," Paul VI defined it as "the wise institution of the Creator," to realize God's design of love within humanity. This "design" for married love, realized in the reciprocal personal gift of self (i.e., sexual intercourse), has two complementary dimensions: (1) mutual personal perfection (the *unitive* meaning) and (2) to collaborate with God in the generation and education of new lives (the *procreative* meaning). The pope went on to outline characteristics that bespeak true "conjugal love." It must be *human*, that is, of the senses and of the spirit at the same time; *total*, that is, the type of personal friendship in which the spouses share everything, without undue reservation; *faithful* and *exclusive* until death; and finally *fecund*, that is, open to new life in cooperation with the Creator of all life.[6]

Following the international Synod on the Family in 1980, John Paul II wrote an apostolic exhortation, *Familiaris Consortio,* in which he, too, presents marriage and conjugal love as a dual-focused reality. Reflecting Paul VI's stated characteristics, John Paul II affirms that true conjugal love "concerns the innermost being of the human person as such. It is realized in a truly human way only if it is an integral part of the love by which a man and a woman commit themselves totally to one another until death."[7] Here and elsewhere he speaks of the inherent "language" or "nuptial meaning" of the body. The physical and psychological bonding that is experienced by spouses through the vulnerability of sexual union bespeaks and incarnates their deeper, underlying, indissoluble marital covenant. Likewise, the procreative dimension of conjugal love is inscribed in the same genital actions by which spouses express, strengthen, and celebrate their unitive love. Thus, the unitive and procreative dimensions of marriage and of conjugal expressions of love form a single whole, a totality that is inseparable.[8]

It then follows that marriage is the only context in which one can rightly give oneself *totally* to another—physically, psychologically, socially, and spiritually—and in which, at the same time, one can remain responsibly open to the procreative possibility of the conjugal act itself. Correlatively, it would be wrong directly to exclude or suppress either divinely ordained meaning of the genital expressions of one's married, covenant love. "One need not

---

6. See *Humanae Vitae*, nos. 8-9, 12.
7. *Familiaris Consortio*, no. 11.
8. See ibid., nos. 11-14, 19-20, 28, 32; *Original Unity of Man and Woman*, pp. 106-112.

always act to realize both of these values, but one may never deliberately suppress either of them."[9] Two broad areas of marital challenge and potential difficulty arise, where the grace of the sacrament of matrimony is especially needed: those related to being faithful to one's permanent commitment and those related to responsible parenthood.

1. Permanent Commitment and Fidelity

As we noted earlier, to say "I love you" and really mean it is no easy task. For love is not only or even primarily a statement about current pleasure, enjoyment, and mutuality. True love, particularly married love, is a pledge for now and for the future, for the unanticipated as well as the foreseeable future. Christians believe that marriage vows are commitments, covenant promises to be there for one's beloved not only for richer, in healthy days, and in the good times, but also to be there for the other in poverty or sickness or worse.

Marriage among baptized Christians constitutes a special sacrament, a Spirit-filled experience. Lived faithfully and well, marriage between Christians, is a real incarnation in the world of the never-ending love of God for humanity, the unconditional love of Christ for his bride, the Church.[10] "The gift of the sacrament is at the same time a vocation and commandment for the Christian spouses, that they may remain faithful to each other forever, beyond every trial and difficulty, in generous obedience to the holy will of the Lord: 'What therefore God has joined together let no [one] put asunder.'"[11]

Honesty, trust, an ability to communicate, an abiding hope, and fidelity, as well as faith in God, are building stones for making marriages last a lifetime. Marital infidelity is always wrong and can never be justified by situational factors. As pastors, we are aware of the pressures weighing on married couples today. The incidence of extramarital sexual affairs or encounters sadly is not uncommon in this country. Christian spouses may find that such a surrounding environment makes their own marital commitment and fidelity more difficult to sustain.[12] The temptation to waver, in an impersonal one-time sexual encounter or in a long-term affair, is not a new human reality, but it does seem to be more common or more commonly accepted in certain sectors of our society today.

---

9. *To Live in Christ Jesus*, no. 46.
10. Cf. *Familiaris Consortio*, nos. 12-13.
11. Ibid., no. 20.
12. See *Faithful to Each Other Forever*, p. 130.

There are steps individuals or couples can take when faced with these challenges and difficulties. They can seek counseling. They can participate in marriage enrichment programs. They can join with other deeply committed couples for nurture and support.

> To all those who in our times consider it too difficult or indeed impossible to be bound to one person for the whole of life, to those caught up in a culture that rejects the indissolubility of marriage and openly mocks the commitment of spouses to fidelity, it is necessary to reconfirm the good news of the definitive nature of that conjugal love that has in Christ its foundation and strength.[13]

In *Faithful to Each Other Forever,* we echo John Paul II in calling for greater "aftercare," pastoral programs and aids for married persons throughout the course of their married life together.[14] Each phase of marriage—the early years; the childbearing years or the no-children years; mid-life crisis and the empty-nest years; senior years; and the inevitable death of one's covenant partner—has its own share of challenges. The Christian Family Movement, Marriage Encounter, parenting groups, family faith-sharing programs, and church-sponsored counseling programs are all to be commended for their commitment to sustaining healthy and holy marriages as well as to helping married persons in trouble.

2a. Responsible Parenthood
Spacing the Birth of Children

Frequently, the term *responsible parenthood* is assumed to be a euphemism for "birth control." While the responsible spacing of children is certainly one dimension of responsible parenthood, we believe such a focus prematurely moves the focus away from the blessing and joy that every child is. Declaring that children are "the supreme gift" and "the ultimate crown" of marriage, the bishops at Vatican II praised those married couples who willingly accept the call to become parents. "Whenever Christian spouses, in a spirit of sacrifice and trust in divine providence, carry out their duties of procreation with generous human and Christian responsibility, they glorify the Creator and perfect themselves in Christ."[15]

In its teaching and pastoral concern for families, the Church emphasizes the need for responsible parenthood. Unfortunately, this term often has been interpreted as a rejection of childbearing.

---

13. *Familiaris Consortio,* no. 20.
14. See *Faithful to Each Other Forever,* pp. 127-138.
15. Austin Flannery, trans., *Pastoral Constitution on the Church in the Modern World,* no. 50.

However, as described by the Second Vatican Council and recent popes, the concept of responsible parenthood involves the following sequential elements:

- a free, informed, mutual decision by the couple regarding the frequency of births and size of the family;

- based on their conscientious assessment of their responsibilities to God, themselves, their children and family, and the society of which they are a part;

- and enlightened by the authentic teaching of the Church's magisterium regarding the objective moral order and the licit methods of spacing or limiting pregnancies.

The challenging, humbling joy expressed by new mothers and fathers as they contemplate the tiny person who is their child finds expression in a number of abstract truths of our Catholic tradition concerning childbearing:

- The conception and birth of every child are something of a miracle.

- Couples possess a remarkable opportunity for cooperating with God in the creation of new human life.

- The one conceived flows out of, manifests, and deepens the spouses' self-giving love for one another.

- The infant is a unique reflection of the singular and special bond between husband and wife—for no other combination of persons could have produced this particular child.

- Parents have the awesome, but challenging, possibility and duty of handing down to their offspring the very Christian faith and positive values given to them by their parents, relatives, community, and Church.

- A child offers the potential for repeated unique moments of tender intimacy and profound satisfaction, continuing throughout many years, that cannot be experienced in any other way.[16]

All this having been said and sincerely believed, still there are decisions to be made concerning the wisdom of procreating at a

---

16. *Faithful to Each Other Forever*, p. 38.

given time or in given circumstances within marriage. Deciding when and whether to act as "cooperators with the love of God the Creator" in procreating new life, a married couple must "reckon with both the material and spiritual conditions of the times as well as of their state in life." Likewise, after consulting the interests of family, society, and the Church, "the parents themselves should ultimately make this judgment, in the sight of God." Finally, in choosing to procreate or to postpone it for a time, spouses "should be aware that they cannot act arbitrarily,"[17] but should make their decisions with prayerful consideration and a spirit of generosity, trusting in divine providence.

For the greater part of this century, the Church has recognized that there are certain times in a married couple's life when sexual intimacy may be desirable, even beneficial to the individuals and to their relationship, at a time when there are sound reasons for wishing to forego pregnancy.[18] In an often quoted *Address to Midwives* (1951), Pius XII taught that for "medical, eugenic, economic and social" reasons a couple may validly forego procreation "for a considerable period of time, even for the entire duration of the marriage."[19] Thus, genuine threats to the life or health of the woman, potential serious genetic deformities for an offspring, the inability to provide financially for the basic needs and education of a child, or some societal inhibition or hindrance are deemed sufficient grounds to forego the procreative dimension of sexual intercourse.

The Church is sensitive to the needs and desires of a couple to space responsibly the birth of children, both for the good of the couple and of the offspring to be born. In keeping with our abiding respect for the inherent procreative meaning of sexual intercourse, it is a teaching of the Catholic Church that one ought to do such spacing "naturally," that is, taking into account the biological ebb and flow of the woman's fertility cycle.

> If, then, there are serious motives to space out births, which derive from the physical or psychological conditions of husband and wife, or from external conditions, the Church teaches that it is then licit [i.e., moral] to take into account the natural rhythms immanent in the generative functions, for the use of marriage in the infecund

---

17. See *Pastoral Constitution on the Church in the Modern World*, no. 50.
18. Cf. Pius XI, *Casti Connubii (On Christian Marriage)*, Encyclical Letter (December 31, 1930), no. 85, as found in Odile M. Liebard, ed., *Official Catholic Teachings: Love and Sexuality* (Wilmington, Del.: McGrath Publishing, 1978), p. 42.
19. Pius XII, *Address to Midwives* (October 29, 1951), no. 301 as found in Liebard, p. 113.

periods only, and in this way to regulate birth without offending the moral principles which have been recalled earlier.[20]

Since a woman is not fertile during the greater part of her menstrual cycle, a couple is respecting the natural "rhythms" ordained by God if they "make use of the infertile periods" for genital love-making, open to the possibility, however unlikely, of a child being conceived.

Natural Family Planning (NFP) traces its roots back to the late 1920s, with the discovery that ovulation precedes the beginning of one's menstrual period by a fairly constant number of days. The subsequent decades have witnessed considerable development in our ability to determine with greater accuracy when a woman is fertile and not fertile. Further scientific study and medical technology have led to a more accurate "multiple-index" approach to calculating the actual time of ovulation in a given menstrual cycle. We recommend strongly that pastoral efforts "be made to render such knowledge accessible to all married people and also to young adults before marriage through clear, timely and serious instruction and education given by married couples, doctors and experts."[21]

> The choice of the natural rhythms involves accepting the cycle of the person, that is, the woman, and thereby accepting dialogue, reciprocal respect, shared responsibility and self-control. To accept the cycle and to enter into dialogue means to recognize both the spiritual and the corporal character of conjugal communion and to live personal love with its requirements of fidelity. In this context the couple comes to experience how conjugal communion is enriched with those values of tenderness and affection which constitute the inner soul of human sexuality in its physical dimension also.[22]

From our pastoral handbook *Faithful to Each Other Forever*, we highlight here five supportive reasons for using Natural Family Planning methods, derived from the experiences of married couples who practice it and professionals who work with them. "Natural family planning:

1. Is comparably effective and much healthier than artificial forms of contraception. . . .

2. Has an holistic sexual approach and orientation. . . .

20. *Humanae Vitae,* no. 16; *Familiaris Consortio,* no. 32.
21. *Familiaris Consortio,* no. 33.
22. Ibid., no. 32.

3. Leads to a greater awareness of each other's bodies. . . .

4. Fosters intimate communication between spouses on a vital subject and encourages the development of diverse, creative ways of expressing affection. . . .

5. Cultivates that type of discipline that both brings joy or satisfaction and simultaneously assists spouses in coping with life's challenges."[23]

In reference to other means of "birth control," the Church teaches that a couple may never, by direct means (i.e., contraceptives), suppress the procreative possibility of sexual intercourse. "Similarly excluded is every action which, either in anticipation of the conjugal act, or in its accomplishment, or in the development of its natural consequences, proposes, whether as an end or as a means, to render procreation impossible."[24] Prohibited are all contraceptive medications, devices, or surgeries that *directly* cause the act of intercourse to be sterile. This includes "the pill," diaphragms, condoms, spermicidal creams, intrauterine devices, and other pre- or postcoital manipulation to prevent conception.

It follows that direct sterilization surgeries (e.g., vasectomies, tubal ligations, hysterectomies), if focused directly on the destruction of one's ability to reproduce, are the most permanent form of contraception. The Church considers this contraceptive means morally wrong because by it, one intends deliberately to suppress the procreative dimension of all future lovemaking. However, if a woman or a man is suffering from a pathological condition, such as ovarian, testicular, or uterine cancer, the Church respects and even recommends the use of the necessary therapeutic means (i.e., direct removal of the diseased organ or tissue), even if, in the process, one is rendered infertile, provided that the infertility is not directly willed.[25]

We hope that the logic of respecting one's natural rhythms expressed here is compelling. We invite those who feel confused or who have genuine doubts about the wisdom of this teaching to read carefully these reflections and the sources cited in the footnotes.

Pastoral sensitivity requires that we be understanding toward those who find it hard to accept this teaching, but it does not permit us to

---

23. *Faithful to Each Other Forever*, pp. 42, 44.
24. *Humanae Vitae*, no. 14.
25. *See ibid., no. 15.*

change or suppress it. . . . At the same time, we urge those who dissent from this teaching of the Church to a prayerful and studied reconsideration of their position.[26]

It is our earnest belief that God's Spirit is working through the magisterium, the authoritative teachers in the Church, in developing this doctrine. To those who, in sincere conscience and after careful study and prayerful reflection, cannot assent to this teaching concerning contraception, we echo Paul VI in assuring them that church ministers and members should respond to them with "patience and goodness, such as the Lord himself gave example of in his dealing with people. Having come not to condemn but to save, he was indeed intransigent with evil, but merciful toward individuals."[27]

John Paul II, in reaffirming the Church's position concerning Natural Family Planning, notes that "the Church is close to the many married couples who find themselves in difficulty over this important point in the moral life. . . . She [the Church] knows that many couples encounter difficulties not only in the concrete fulfillment of the moral norm but even in understanding its inherent values."[28] As teachers, charged with the task of preserving and passing on the truth of the tradition, we applaud those couples who deliberately and generously decide to act as co-creators with God in the miracle of new life. For those couples who have serious reasons for avoiding or postponing pregnancy, we reaffirm the Church's stand for Natural Family Planning, and against artificial means of contraception. As pastors, may we embody compassion and the abiding care of a loving parent toward all those who seek the truth with a sincere heart.[29]

2b. Responsible Parenthood
Reproductive Technology

Responsible parenthood is for some a question of spacing or forestalling conception (i.e., the birth-control issue), but for many couples the personal and ethical dilemmas are quite the opposite. We feel deep compassion and empathy for those married couples who find themselves unable to conceive or bear children. To dispel the myth that the Church sees marriage solely or primarily in terms

---

26. *To Live in Christ Jesus*, no. 49.
27. *Humanae Vitae*, no. 29.
28. *Familiaris Consortio*, no. 33.
29. Cf. ibid.; *Faithful to Each Other Forever*, p. 46.

of procreating children, we quote from the Vatican II document, *Pastoral Constitution on the Church in the Modern World:*

> Marriage to be sure is not instituted solely for procreation. Rather, its nature as an unbreakable compact between persons, and the welfare of the children, both demand that the mutual love of the spouses, too, be embodied in a rightly ordered manner, that it grow and ripen. Therefore, marriage persists as a whole manner and communion of life, and maintains its value and indissolubility, even when offspring are lacking—despite, rather often, the very intense desire of the couple.[30]

The Church long has recognized that the sacramental bond of marriage exists wherever a Christian man and woman pledge covenant fidelity for the whole of life, regardless of whether they are past childbearing age or are unable to conceive children naturally. Such couples should feel no shame or stigma because their covenant love endures and is creative in ways distinct from biological parenthood. Adoption is certainly a commendable option. Accepting children conceived and borne by others as one's own is a special calling requiring special grace. Adoptive parents reflect, in a unique way, the parental relationship of God with each of us as Jesus' adoptive sisters and brothers.[31] Likewise, many childless couples find great satisfaction in sharing their time and talent in service to their wider family or in community outreach. The ways and means of being "creative" and loving extend far beyond the nursery and biological parenthood.

However, the desire for a child is a natural one. Children are one of the key privileges and blessings of a fruitful marriage. This desire may be acutely felt by the couple who is affected by sterility, particularly if normal fertility therapy indicates it may be irreparable. "Nevertheless, marriage does not confer on the spouses the right to have a a child, but only the right to perform those natural acts which are *per se* ordered to procreation."[32]

Early in 1987, the Vatican Congregation for the Doctrine of the Faith issued its *Instruction on Respect for Human Life in Its Origin and on the Dignity of Procreation,* a document that deals at great length with the ethical questions related to reproductive technologies: artificial insemination, *in vitro* fertilization, surrogate motherhood, and so on. The document distinguished between what is "techni-

---

30. *Pastoral Constitution on the Church in the Modern World*, no. 50.
31. Cf. Romans 8:14-17, 9:4; Galatians 4:5; Ephesians 1:5.
32. Congregation for the Doctrine of the Faith, *Instruction on Respect for Human Life in Its Origin and on the Dignity of Procreation: Replies to Certain Questions of the Day* (February 22, 1987), quotation from Part IIB, no. 8.

cally possible"—what one *can do*—and what is "morally admissible"—what one *ought to* or *may do*.

The Church's approach to artificial aids to procreation is grounded in two fundamental values: (1) protecting the life and dignity of the human being so created, and (2) the conviction that the transmission of life ought to occur through marital intercourse. "For this reason one cannot use means and follow methods which could be licit in the transmission of the life of plants and animals."[33]

While every infant conceived, by whatever procedure, is to be accepted and treasured as a gift from God, from an ethical viewpoint, the "end" (wanting a baby) does not justify any and all "means" (by methods other than conjugal lovemaking). No one has an absolute right to have a child. In order to preserve "the unity of the human being and the dignity of one's origin" as well as the linkage between the unitive and procreative dimensions of marital lovemaking, we believe that procreation remains fully human only when it is brought about "as the fruit of the conjugal act specific to the love between spouses."[34]

The term *heterologous* is used to designate all artificial fertilization involving ova, sperm, gametes, or the organs of a third party, someone other than the married couple. This includes artificial insemination using donor sperm, *in vitro* fertilization using donor sperm or ova, and the use of a surrogate mother's womb to carry an infant to term. The 1987 document argues that this introduction of a third person or that person's bodily tissue or organs into the conception of a couple's child "is contrary to the unity of marriage, to the dignity of the spouses, to the vocation proper to parents, and to the child's right to be conceived and brought into the world in marriage and from marriage."[35]

Homologous artificial fertilization refers to those reproductive procedures in which the sperm and ovum belong solely to the parents of the infant-to-be (*in vitro* fertilization using the couple's sperm/ovum or artificial insemination using the husband's sperm only). The Church teaches that separating conception from the conjugal "act" severs the unitive and procreative linkage that ought to exist in every human act of conception.

For a fuller treatment of these complex biomedical issues, we recommend recourse to the full text of the document cited here. Whatever its cause or prognosis, infertility is certainly a difficult

---

33. Ibid., Introduction, no. 4.
34. Ibid., Part IIB, no. 4.
35. Ibid., Part IIA, no. 2.

trial. We call on all pastoral ministers and the whole community of believers to be supportive of couples who anguish over the issue of infertility. We commend professional counselors and pastoral care-givers involved in helping couples deal with their own self-esteem, feelings, and sense of loss. Catholic social service agencies deserve high praise for their adoption programs, which, for many childless couples and orphan children, offer loving matches. We encourage scientists to continue their research into the causes, prevention, and remedy for infertility, with a rightful caution that proposed procedures ought to respect both the inherent good of the infant to be conceived and the conjugal integrity of the spouses involved.

Sexuality and the Single Person

There is no simple definition for the single life. The term *single* represents a wide variety of life-styles in our culture: those transitionally and those permanently single; those once married who now are separated, divorced, or widowed. There are single people in the urban, suburban, and rural context; persons single by preference, as well as those single because of "circumstances."[36] Singles who have never married may be single because they choose to remain so. Sometimes, they are presently single because they simply have not met the right marriage partner yet. Often, separated or divorced people are single "again" because marital strife or abuse has led to separate living situations. Singles widowed by the death of a spouse may or may not choose to marry again.[37]

There was a time, earlier in this century and in centuries past, when marriages took place early in life, shortly after the onset of puberty, and such marriages enjoyed the support of the wider society. With the advent of greater personal, educational, and career freedom for women as well as men, the median age for marriage has been pushed back, often to one's early twenties or beyond. For better and worse, there can be a full decade or longer gap between the time when biological sexual urges dawn and the time when a person chooses to marry.

Chastity, for the single person, is not synonymous with an interior calling to perpetual celibacy. Controlling one's desires for

---

36. See Department of Education, USCC, *The Single Experience: A Resource,* Reflections and Models for Single Young Adulthood (Washington, D.C.: USCC Office for Publishing and Promotion Services, 1979). Quotation from Rev. Patrick O'Neill, OSA, "Overview."
37. See Kay Ellen Kramer, "Singleness: A Challenge to the Church," in *The Single Experience: A Resource,* p. 3.

sexual intimacy can be particularly difficult. Being single in a largely couples' society is not an easy calling, whether it be temporary or permanent. Societal stereotypes regarding the single life abound. Some presume that single people are sadly incomplete and unfulfilled without a mate. Others stereotype the single lifestyle as carefree. Thus, single adults are sometimes imposed upon to carry more than their fair share of family or social burdens. A mature single person seeks a careful balance between a healthy independence, with a reasonable degree of privacy and freedom, and the need for love, including genuine intimacy and community "belonging."[38]

Those who choose single life as the means to live out their Christian calling, as well as those who accept singleness in the present, open to whatever the future may bring, can find a model *par excellence* in Jesus Christ. During his life on earth, he was a single person. Single people testify to the fact that our God-given purpose and destiny incorporate but are not synonymous with one's marital status. Single women and men can, and many do, live deeply happy, whole, and holy lives.

Loneliness and intimacy are realities that every human being must strive to balance. Single people can and do commit themselves in a variety of intimate, that is, close and loving, relationships. One's parental family may be a special source of joy and challenge to a single adult. Co-workers, peers, and friends invite single people to love and be loved as members of wider networks or "family-type" groupings. So also, single men and women bring their talents and dedication to their jobs or professions, to the Church, to community organizations, and to the wider society.

Despite this variety of relationships and commitments, there are lonely times with which single people must cope. Sometimes, these are moments of uncertainty and extreme pain. One may feel a sense of isolation. We have listened to and empathize with the particular pains associated with singleness. We suggest that these are potentially fruitful times, even if not particularly happy times. In these moments of loneliness one can encounter God, face to face as it were, if he or she will "let go," trusting that God is there. While God is tangibly present in life's moments of intimacy, the divine presence also can be experienced powerfully in life's moments of loneliness.[39] So, for single people, there is a particular need to

---

38. See Kathy Szaj, "To Whom Do I Belong? Where Are My People?" in *The Single Experience: A Resource*, p. 17.
39. See Keith Clark, *An Experience of Celibacy* (Notre Dame: Ave Maria Press, 1982).

balance life's moments of loneliness with life's moments of intimacy.

Loneliness or the yearning to love and to be loved can call us forth, challenging us to rekindle existing bonds or to seek and find new ones. The love of family and true friends can reassure us that we are loved and empower our own ability to love and make new commitment. We are and remain sexual beings, whatever our state in life.

Still, the Church teaches that genital sexual union "is only legitimate if a definitive community of life [i.e., marriage] has been established between the man and the woman."[40] Participation in nonmarital sex violates an objective moral norm, which the Church teaches, and is not an acceptable way to live chastely as a single adult.[41] In the previous chapter, and in the section on conjugal love earlier in this chapter, we noted that this moral norm is grounded in the Church's teaching that the unitive and procreative dimensions of sexual lovemaking, by their very nature, require a *total* commitment of the participants in order for them to reflect their full, divinely intended meaning.

Much is written and discussed today about the phenomenon of *cohabitation* between the sexes. Nonmarital sexual intercourse and living together without marriage are not identical issues or questions. "Couples may engage in sexual intercourse without living together; other couples, particularly those sharing homes for financial reasons, might live together without having sexual intercourse."[42] While cohabitation, by definition, does not necessarily involve genital sexual intimacy, it does establish a situation in which avoidance of nonmarital sex becomes exceptionally difficult, particularly for those couples bound by affection or even contemplating marriage. When two people move in together without exchanging formal wedding vows and live "externally as husband and wife," they can create more difficulties for themselves and can cause a potential scandal for others by weakening the sanctity and respect society has for marriage itself. In addition, empirical data raises doubts about cohabitation as a healthy or helpful preparation for married life.[43] For these reasons, we do not believe that cohabitation that simulates marriage is appropriate

---

40. *Declaration on Certain Questions Concerning Sexual Ethics,* no. 7.
41. See *Faithful to Each Other Forever,* p. 71.
42. Ibid.
43. See ibid., pp. 71-77; this is a very helpful reflection on the topic of *cohabitation.*

behavior for Catholics or others seeking to live a Christian way of life.

Finally, we express our deep appreciation for the presence of so many Catholic single adults in the church community. Many of them offer time and talent both to parish activities and to the wider vocation of being Christ's image in the modern world, in the marketplace, and in the professions. We realize that too often they may feel left out, without a distinctive "theology" of the single state alongside theologies of marriage and theologies of religious life and vowed celibacy. For some, their decision to be and remain single is indeed a chosen and Spirit-filled calling. Other single adults are in transition, neither contentedly "unmarried" nor avowedly celibate and single. We gently remind them that chastity is a virtue that demands fidelity, a sexually appropriate response from each person. We encourage diocesan leaders and religious educators to be more attuned to the presence, needs, and talents of all single people in the local parish and church community. Following the Synod on the Laity in 1987, John Paul II wrote a special document, *On the Vocation and Mission of the Lay Faithful in the World*, that speaks well to some of these concerns.[44]

Persons with a Homosexual Orientation

Sexuality, as noted earlier, is a fundamental dimension of every human being. It is reflected physiologically, psychologically, and relationally in a person's gender identity as well as in one's primary sexual orientation and behavior. For some young men and women, this means a discovery that one is homosexual, that is, that one's "sexual inclinations are oriented predominantly toward persons of the same sex."[45] Other persons experience a bisexual orientation. These orientations involve one's feelings and sexual fantasies as well as one's overtly sexual and genital actions.

In recent decades, a distinction has been drawn between persons whose homosexual orientation seems to be transitory—the result of education, environment, or adolescent habit—and those persons for whom homosexuality is a permanent, seemingly irreversible

---

44. John Paul II, *On the Vocation and Mission of the Lay Faithful in the World* (*Christifideles Laici*), Apostolic Exhortation (December 30, 1988).
45. National Conference of Catholic Bishops, *Principles to Guide Confessors in Questions of Homosexuality* (Washington, D.C.: USCC Office for Publishing and Promotion Services, 1973), p. 3.

sexual orientation. The medical and behavioral sciences do not as yet know what causes a person to be homosexual. Whether it is related to genetics, hormones, or some variation in psychosocial upbringing, the scientific data presently seems inconclusive. There may be a combination of factors involved.

Mindful of the inherent and abiding dignity of every human person, we reaffirm what we wrote in 1976, namely, that "homosexual [persons], like everyone else, should not suffer from prejudice against their basic human rights. They have a right to respect, friendship, and justice. They should have an active role in the Christian community."[46] We echo strongly the Congregation for the Doctrine of the Faith, which, in a 1986 document, stated, "It is deplorable that homosexual persons have been and are the object of violent malice in speech or in action. Such treatment deserves condemnation from the Church's pastors wherever it occurs."[47]

We call on all Christians and citizens of good will to confront their own fears about homosexuality and to curb the humor and discrimination that offend homosexual persons. We understand that having a homosexual orientation brings with it enough anxiety, pain, and issues related to self-acceptance without society adding additional prejudicial treatment.

However, we also want to express clearly the Church's teaching that "homosexual [genital] activity, as distinguished from homosexual orientation, is morally wrong."[48] Such an orientation in itself, because not freely chosen, is not sinful.[49] As we have stated several times in this document, we believe that it is only within a heterosexual marital relationship that genital sexual activity is morally acceptable. Only within marriage does sexual intercourse fully symbolize the Creator's dual design, as an act of covenant love, with the potential of co-creating new human life. Therefore, homosexual genital activity is considered immoral. Like heterosexual persons, homosexual men and women are called to give witness to chastity, avoiding, with God's grace, behavior that is wrong for them, just as nonmarital sexual relations are wrong for heterosexual men and women.[50]

---

46. *To Live in Christ Jesus*, no. 52.
47. *Letter to the Bishops of the Catholic Church on the Pastoral Care of Homosexual Persons*, no. 10.
48. *To Live in Christ Jesus*, no. 52.
49. See *Letter to the Bishops of the Catholic Church on the Pastoral Care of Homosexual Persons*, no. 3: "Although the particular inclination of the homosexual person is not a sin, it is a more or less strong tendency ordered toward an intrinsic moral evil; and thus the inclination itself must be seen as an objective disorder." Here, two things must be noted. To speak of the homosexual *inclination* as "objectively disordered" does not mean that the homosexual *person* as such is evil or bad. Furthermore, the homosexual person is not the only one who has disordered tendencies or inclinations. All human beings are subject to some disordered tendencies.
50. See *To Live in Christ Jesus*, no. 52.

In the pastoral field, we reaffirm that homosexual men and women "must certainly be treated with understanding" and sustained in Christian hope.[51] Their moral responsibility ought to be judged with a degree of prudence. Parents, teachers, confessors, and the whole "Christian community should offer a special degree of pastoral understanding and care," particularly since having a homosexual orientation generally precludes a person from entering marriage.[52]

Living as a chaste homosexual person is not an easy way of life, particularly if one feels drawn to live a commitment with another person. The Church challenges homosexual men and women to join "whatever sufferings and difficulties they experience in virtue of their condition to the sacrifice of the Lord's cross."[53] This is not to be seen merely as pointless self-denial. Rather, following the way of the cross is the way of virtue, of becoming a mature, sexually appropriate, chaste person, in service to the will of God.

Educationally, homosexuality cannot and ought not to be skirted or ignored. The topic "must be faced in all objectivity by the pupil and the educator when the case presents itself."[54] First and foremost, we support modeling and teaching respect for every human person, regardless of sexual orientation. Second, a parent or teacher must also present clearly and delicately the unambiguous moral norms of the Christian tradition regarding homosexual genital activity, appropriately geared to the age level and maturity of the learner. Finally, parents and other educators must remain open to the possibility that a particular person, whether adolescent or adult, may be struggling to accept his or her own homosexual orientation. The distinction between *being* homosexual and *doing* homosexual genital actions, while not always clear and convincing, is a helpful and important one when dealing with the complex issue of homosexuality, particularly in the educational and pastoral arena.

Vowed or Professed Celibacy

As part of this chapter devoted to special groups and particular sexual expressions, it is appropriate to speak briefly about those dedicated people who have accepted the call to live as celibates "for

---

51. See *Declaration on Certain Questions Concerning Sexual Ethics*, no. 8.
52. *To Live in Christ Jesus*, no. 52.
53. *Letter to the Bishops of the Catholic Church on the Pastoral Care of Homosexual Persons*, no. 12.
54. *Educational Guidance in Human Love*, no. 101.

the sake of the kingdom." We express our gratitude for the commitment of those men and women who have taken vows or made solemn promises to live a celibate vocation. "The *theory* of celibacy poses no huge problem. The celibate chooses not to give his [her] life to any one person, so as to be able to share it generously with many people. That's the ideal."[55] Celibacy is an intense, personal, special type of life with God that comes from the depth of our womanhood/manhood.

However, ordination, a vow, or a promise does not neutralize the role of sexuality in a person's life. Priests or religious sisters and brothers retain their entire incarnate being, including gender identity and sexual feelings. In *practice,* living out the commitment to forego the experience of conjugal love can be very difficult. Because celibate persons are called to love and serve all the people whose lives they touch, young and old, men and women, their vocation, like that of all Christians, is one of being fully human and fully alive. They are called to relate to others authentically and deeply in friendship. It is the question of giving appropriate expression to such friendship that is, at times, troublesome. Finding the median between chaste embodied expressions of care and affection and those reserved to couples moving toward marital commitment calls for careful and candid discernment. As celibates, we admit that we "don't find celibate life-sharing an easy task; we have to keep working at it and renewing our resolves, learning from our mistakes."[56]

As we noted in speaking about living as a single person, one of the common experiences that accompanies being unmarried is a special degree or kind of loneliness that may accompany the absence of a spouse and children. Some priests and vowed religious seek to fill in this gap by plunging headlong into ministerial activity. Every fruitful pastoral minister knows that there are interpersonal rewards—love, joy, and unique kinds of intimacy—that derive from being involved in the lives of others. In this way, celibates give effective witness to the God of love. However, we caution that "workaholism," as distinct from healthy work habits, is no long-term solution for the loneliness that, at times, accompanies the celibate life-style. Depression, substance abuse, or other aberrant behavior can result if celibate men and women do not deal

---

55. Bishops' Committee on Priestly Life and Ministry, NCCB, *A Reflection Guide on Human Sexuality and the Ordained Priesthood* (Washington, D.C.: USCC Office for Publishing and Promotion Services, 1983), p. 43.
56. Ibid., pp. 8 and 43.

honestly and in a balanced manner with their own sexual feelings and interpersonal needs.[57]

To live celibate love chastely in a society that espouses a largely secular and sex-oriented value system is not easy.

> But neither is the living of conjugal chastity within the exalted vocation of Christian marriage. Hence, Christian life, married or unmarried, requires the discipline of Christian chastity to be lived in a fully Christian way. When that discipline is self-imposed and chosen by the priest [or sister or brother] in the context of the charism of celibacy, it can flower in a unique kind of spiritual growth and a unique unfolding of the life of the Spirit.[58]

John Paul II suggests that virginity or celibacy, accepted for the sake of the kingdom, serves as a complement to the vocation of marriage. "Marriage and virginity or celibacy are two ways of expressing and living the one mystery of the covenant of God with his people."[59] If marriage and conjugal love were not valuable, a great blessing, then the choice to forego that pathway would not be considered such a sacrifice.

Adolescence in the 1990s
A Special Challenge

No chapter that discusses individuals or groups facing difficult sexual decisions would be complete without some mention of today's adolescents. Young people in the early 1990s are challenged to mature in a culture that is not only different, but in many ways more complex and difficult than the one in which their parents and grandparents were raised. "It is an environment at times hostile to Christian values and often exploitive in the way it treats other human beings."[60]

Adolescence, that somewhat awkward period between the onset of puberty and adulthood, is an exciting and important time for young people. Internal chemical and biological changes trigger powerful, seemingly uncontrollable emotional responses, strong yearnings to be loved, to be needed, to be accepted. It is a time in

---

57. Cf. *Educational Guidance in Human Love*, no. 31; Matthew 22:23-33; Mark 12:18-27; Luke 20:27-40. Further helpful reflections on *celibacy* can be found in these ecclesial documents and in annual Holy Thursday papal reflections on priesthood: *Pastoral Constitution on the Church in the Modern World*, Part II, Ch. 1; Paul VI, *Encyclical Letter on Priestly Celibacy* (June 24, 1967); *Familiaris Consortio*, no. 16.
58. *A Reflection Guide on Human Sexuality and the Ordained Priest*, p. 11.
59. *Familiaris Consortio*, no. 16.
60. Pennsylvania Catholic Conference, *To Love and to Be Loved: The Pennsylvania Catholic Bishops Speak to Youth on the Gift of Sexuality* (January 1989), p. 2.

which adolescents begin to experience their potential to reach out in love to others.

As they experience the stress of many concurrent changes in their lives—physical, emotional, psychological, and relational—and the challenges that accompany such dramatic change, there can emerge tremendous self-doubts and personal insecurity. Vague feelings and thoughts lead to threshold questions such as: "Who am I?" "Am I normal?" Am I worth having as a friend?" "Who or what can I trust?" "What do I believe in?" "Who cares about *me*?" Adolescence is a period in their lives when young people need affirmation, love, respect, care, and concern.[61] They need a special measure of acceptance and support as they strive to acquire for themselves a healthy identity as a male or female person.

We can understand and empathize with their confusion in an American culture plagued with double standards. On the one hand, nonmarital and extramarital sexual affairs are portrayed in much of the media as acceptable, even commendable. On the other hand, political candidates and elected officials are cast aside or hounded out of office because of similar sexual activity.[62] At the same time, adolescents are bombarded "by the advertising industry, which so often takes advantage of the erotic in order to sell its products and by the phenomenon of peer pressure, which exercises such strong influence on teenagers who may be physically mature but still are lacking in emotional and psychological maturity."[63]

How, then, amidst this late twentieth-century climate, do adolescents prepare themselves for maturity? There are no easy shortcuts. "Young people must come to terms with the dramatic changes their bodies are undergoing, with powerful new feelings that accompany this change, with desires whose potential is life changing and sometimes life threatening, with new concerns about the consequences of one's actions and with the moral dimensions of adult life."[64] While integrating all the dimensions of one's self is a lifelong process for every person, for most of us, there is no more challenging, often confusing period than the teen years. Young people need and deserve to hear and see modeled for them the positive moral values that good parents, society at its best, and the Church profess.

Quite understandably, parents or guardians worry about their

61. See Archbishop John Roach, *Grateful for the Gift: Sexuality, Parents and Teens* (March 1988), as printed in *Origins* (March 17, 1988): 690.
62. See *To Love and to Be Loved*, pp. 7-8.
63. Massachusetts Catholic Conference, *Sex Education: Information or Formation?* (November 20, 1987), as printed in *Origins* (December 31, 1987): 510.
64. *Grateful for the Gift*, p. 691.

children at the onset of puberty. Keeping teens in school, off alcohol and other drugs, safe when driving, involved with the "right crowd," and not sexually active or pregnant—these are some of the concerns contemporary parents must face. While children learn from many others—teachers, older siblings, ministers, counselors, peers, and media personalities—still, parents teach children the most in life. "From the cradle to the grave, we compare what we know to what our parents know."[65] In their role as primary teachers and models for young people, parents and guardians deserve the strong support of their churches, their children's schools, and the society at large. Through our combined efforts, we can help young people develop healthier attitudes toward themselves and others, and a sense of responsibility about their own choices and actions.

Because of limited life experience, as well as their own tentative grasp on the meaning of their pubescent experiences, adolescents often find serious talk about relationships and about sexuality to be difficult, certainly awkward. It is precisely at these times that "sexual activity can distract young persons and hinder them from the hard work involved with this task of developing good communication skills."[66] Few adolescents have attained sufficient freedom or the maturity to express feelings well, to act on them wisely, and to keep peer pressure in perspective. The adolescent years are a time of growth, a period of sorting out relationships among family and friends. Quite simply, in the midst of this self-identity quest, few if any adolescents have sufficient energy or resources to be someone else's committed partner or mate.

At this key time in the process of growing up, adolescent sexual involvement considerably reduces the time, energy, and attention needed for personal development. This development comes through forming a variety of friendships with many persons. These friendships and different personal contacts are very important for a young person developing a sense of self-esteem and discovering what matters to him or her, what is really important in life. "Sexual involvement at this time usually means an unhealthy emotional dependence on one person, just when a successful maturing process requires having many and different kinds of contacts and friendships with others."[67]

It is on the basis of this broader experience in evaluating people that adolescents eventually will be able to make permanent com-

---

65. Ibid., p. 690.
66. *Faithful to Each Other Forever*, p. 35.
67. *To Love and to Be Loved*, p. 5.

mitments. As stated earlier, the Church teaches that it is only when a person commits oneself to a partner in marriage that there is enough assurance for both that the physical gift of self in sex is meant to be complete and lasting, in accordance with God's plan. "Youthful relationships tend to be intense, short-lived, and numerous. When there is an ultimate, even if immature, gift of heart and body in such experiences, the subsequent breakup of the relationship and the rejection connected with it can bruise terribly the person's self-esteem and cause serious psychological damage."[68]

Many young people today consider genital sexual activity, including intercourse, to be acceptable behavior, a "right" of sorts, even outside the context of marriage. However, the Catholic tradition affirms that genital sexual intimacy, particularly intercourse, is a right and privilege reserved to those who have committed themselves for life in marriage. It is only in the context of the marital covenant that genital sex finds its full meaning as an embodied expression of the intimacy and fidelity of the couple. We urge parents and teachers to insist on sexual abstinence and preparation for marital responsibility for adolescents. We believe this to be inscribed in our human nature as well as in the Christian call from God. Adults who guide adolescents in their moral development need to be forthright and clear in this regard, acknowledging and supporting the courage it may require from young people.

We are convinced that we must be more positive in our description of abstinence. For too many people, it means "going without," and that is too myopic a view. "Abstinence should be thought of not just as a no to sexual activity, but also as a yes to one's future and to one's future spouse. It is a yes to one's own inner potential, to one's ability to love and to express love. It is a yes to trust, faithfulness and friendship."[69]

At the same time that we recommend a strong stand in behalf of sexual abstinence for adolescents, we also need to assure them, "God understands better than any human being the difficulties and powerful urges" with which they are dealing. The supportive love of God, reflected in the life of Jesus, "reassures us that even when we are weak and fail, the Lord's compassion and forgiveness are always there."[70] Through prayer, discipline, and the grace of the sacraments, every person can overcome the temptation to sin. It is important to keep mistakes in perspective. We must forgive our-

---

68. *Faithful to Each Other Forever*, p. 35.
69. *Grateful for the Gift*, p. 691.
70. *To Love and to Be Loved*, p. 8.

selves, even as God forgives us, and start again. "Growing up is never a straight line—it is far worse to lose our values than it is to make a mistake."[71]

A Few Overarching Issues

Before concluding this chapter, we wish to speak briefly about four sexuality-related issues that are the sole concern of no individual group treated above: (1) masturbation; (2) art versus pornography; (3) the HIV Infection/AIDS Crisis; and (4) sexual abuse and dysfunction.

1. Masturbation

The Catholic tradition has consistently held that autoerotic or solitary genital sexual behavior is immoral and, in the objective sphere, can never be ethically justified. Recall that the Church teaches that sexual orgasm ought to be linked to marital intercourse, which, by definition, serves both lovemaking and lifegiving purposes. It follows that masturbation is not procreative, nor is it unitive in any interpersonal sense. This is not intended to deny the psychological or sociological data, which indicate that such behavior is common, especially among the young. Modern behavioral sciences provide us with much valid and useful information for formulating better contextual judgments and more sensitive pastoral responses. As one Vatican document puts it:

> Psychology helps one to see how the immaturity of adolescence (which can sometimes persist after that age), psychological imbalance or habit can influence behavior, diminishing the deliberate character of the act and bringing about a situation whereby subjectively there may not always be serious fault. But in general, the absence of serious responsibility must not be presumed.[72]

From an educational and pastoral viewpoint, it is valuable to consider that masturbation may be a symptom of underlying psychological and interpersonal difficulties that provoke a certain amount of tension that the person seeks to release through these actions. Pedagogical efforts and pastoral care should be focused on the development of the whole person, seeing these actions in context, seeking their underlying causes more than seeking to repress the actions in isolation.[73]

---

71. *Grateful for the Gift*, p. 692.
72. *Declaration on Certain Questions Concerning Sexual Ethics*, no. 9.
73. See *Educational Guidance in Human Love*, no. 99.

In order to help an adolescent learner "to feel accepted in a communion of charity and freed from self-enclosure," a parent, teacher, or counselor "should undramatize masturbation and not reduce his or her esteem and benevolence" for the person. We encourage all educators and counselors to help those who masturbate to move toward better social integration, to be more open and interested in others, in order eventually to be free from this form of behavior. Thus, they will advance toward the kind of interpersonal love proper to mature affectivity. At the same time, we encourage people who struggle with masturbation "to have recourse to the recommended means of Christian asceticism, such as prayer and the sacraments, and to be involved in works of justice and charity."[74]

2. Art versus Pornography

Throughout history, the Church has been a patron of the arts. From the sculptures and paintings of masters like Leonardo da Vinci and Michelangelo to the haunting melodies of Gregorian chant and the intricate harmonies of Palestrina's Masses, the Catholic tradition has supported creativity that celebrates the human soul, delights our embodied senses, and gives glory to God the Creator. However, in the name of artistic license and, in this country, under the banner of First Amendment free speech, an industry has arisen that uses the arts of filmmaking, painting, photography, and the printed word more to exploit and degrade human sensitivities than to uplift them.

Pornography, the use of visual or print media to present nudity and sexual activity in a degrading or depersonalizing way, often preys upon the most vulnerable in our society. Women, children, and men all too often are portrayed as objects at the disposal of the sexual lust or violent actions of others. Children, too, can find ready access to materials that may warp their view of women or men, of sexuality, and of the mutual love and responsibility that rightly ought to accompany sexual intimacy.

We urge writers, artists, actors, designers, producers, exhibitors, distributors, operators, sellers, critics, and whoever else may have a part in making and transmitting products of communication to accept their access to the airwaves and to the public as a societal trust. We challenge them to use their skills effectively, creatively, and humanely for the common good. May profit alone, the unbri-

---

74. Ibid., no. 100; *Declaration on Certain Questions Concerning Sexual Ethics*, no. 9.

dled law of supply and demand, never dictate their art or craft. They have the ability and the awesome responsibility to help mold and channel public opinion and social morality.[75]

By portraying men, women, and children respectfully, they can foster a greater appreciation among us, one for another. Yes, the dark side of humanity ought rightfully to find expression in the arts, but always with a critical eye, a questioning presentation, lest the glamour of evil seduce an unsuspecting viewer or reader. "Whether it be a question of artistic or literary works, public entertainment or providing information, each individual in his or her own domain must show tact, discretion, moderation and a true sense of values."[76]

In everyday life, the instruments of social communication—television, film, videos, radio, magazines, newspapers, music—by their intrusiveness and repetitive suggestion, impress on all of us, particularly teenagers and children, "a continuous and conditioning stream of information and training."[77] Consequently, special duties bind all of us as consumers—readers, viewers, and listeners—to be discerning in our selection of media, for ourselves and for those entrusted to us. As a society, we have the right as well as the responsibility to monitor the public airwaves and media outlets.

We neither accept the assertion that "What is pornography to one is the laughter of genius to another" nor do we fall back on the often quoted vague assertion "I know it when I see it."[78] Aware that community standards have, at times, been too puritanical and restrictive, we fear that the opposite extreme—a misguided permissiveness, in the name of artistic license and free speech—currently may hold sway in this country. Working together, we can create communities where the arts can flourish, free speech is respected, and pornography finds no tolerance.

3. The HIV Infection/AIDS Crisis

No document on issues related to sexuality in our times would be complete without some mention of the disease known as AIDS (Acquired Immunodeficiency Syndrome). HIV infection (Human Immunodeficiency Virus), in all its forms, is an insidious illness

---

75. See Vatican Council II, *Decree on the Instruments of Social Communication* (December 4, 1963), no. 11.
76. *Declaration on Certain Questions Concerning Sexual Ethics*, no. 13.
77. *Educational Guidance in Human Love*, nos. 66-68, quotation from no. 66.
78. D. H. Lawrence, *Women In Love*; Justice Potter Stewart, as quoted in Vincent Barry, "Pornography," in *Applying Ethics* (Belmont, Calif.: Wadsworth, 1985), p. 91.

because it attacks the body's own immune system, leaving one defenseless, open to a variety of infections and other complications. At the time we are writing this document, there is no cure for AIDS. It is a fatal illness. However, some inroads have been made in developing drug therapies to treat some of its symptoms and to slow its progress. This is a disease that cuts across all socioeconomic, ethnic, and cultural boundaries.

HIV infection can be transmitted in a variety of ways. It is transferred by body fluids from one person to another. Thus, one avenue for the transmission of the virus is sexual contact with someone who already is a carrier (HIV positive) or who is a person with AIDS. By urging premarital chastity and marital fidelity, Catholic moral teaching provides the best means of avoiding AIDS. IV drug users who share needles are likewise susceptible to contracting the virus if their needle partners are carriers or persons with AIDS. Tainted blood supplies could also infect blood recipients, though the introduction of proper screening techniques has greatly reduced the risk of contracting HIV infection through routine blood transfusions. Also, pregnant women who are carriers of the virus can infect their infants *in utero* through the intermingling of body fluids. AIDS is therefore a human disease, not restricted to any one group or subsection of society nor to any lone means of transmission.

We believe that it is wrong to speak of HIV infection as any sort of "divine retribution" or to label its victims in any sense as "deserving" such a disease. Jesus confronted such a linkage between sin as cause and disease as effect when he told the crowd that the man born blind was not disabled because of his own sin nor that of his parents.[79] Jesus Christ, the perfect incarnation of God, came to heal, to comfort, and to save. It would seem contrary to the image of God reflected in the life of Jesus and New Testament revelation to heap abuse or harsh judgment on those who suffer HIV infection. Ministry to the sick and dying—incarnated in hospitals, nursing homes, hospice programs, and other health care services—has been a long-standing characteristic and commitment of the Christian tradition.

The thousands of persons who have died from this as yet incurable disease give all of us pause. We express our genuine sympathy for those who currently are persons with AIDS or who have tested HIV positive. We empathize with their families, loved ones, and

---

79. See John 9:1-41.

friends. We, too, are touched by the magnitude of lives lost in our own families, among our fellow ministers, and in our various dioceses. Our reflections, in brief, may be summarized in this way:

1. AIDS is an illness to which all must respond in a manner consistent with the best medical and scientific information available.

2. As members of the Church and society, we must reach out with compassion to those exposed to or experiencing this disease and must stand in solidarity with them and their families.

3. As bishops, we must offer a clear presentation of Catholic moral teaching concerning human intimacy and sexuality.

4. Discrimination and violence against persons with AIDS and with HIV infection are unjust and immoral.

5. Social realities like poverty and oppression and psychological factors like loneliness and alienation can strongly influence people's decisions to behave in ways which expose them to the AIDS virus.

6. Along with other groups in society, the Church must work to eliminate the harsh realities of poverty and despair.

7. The expression of human sexuality should resemble God's love in being loving, faithful, and committed. Human sexuality in marriage is intrinsically oriented to permanent commitment, love, and openness to new life.

8. The spread of AIDS will not be halted unless people live in accord with authentic human values pertaining to personhood and sexuality.

9. Since AIDS can be transmitted through intravenous drug use, there is need for drug treatment programs, a halt to traffic in illicit drugs, and efforts to eliminate the causes of addiction.

10. Considering the widespread ignorance and misunderstanding about HIV infection and its modes of transmission, educational programs about the medical aspects of the disease and legitimate ways of preventing it are also needed.[80]

4. Sexual Abuse and Dysfunction

In recent years, we, as a Church and as a society, have become more aware of the alarming number of cases of child sexual molestation in our communities. Whether the problem is more acute today, or whether we just are becoming more socially conscious of it, there is no justification, moral or otherwise, for the use of children as objects for genital pleasure, as victims of adult anger

---

80. National Conference of Catholic Bishops, *Called to Compassion and Responsibility: A Response to the HIV/AIDS Crisis* (Washington, D.C.: USCC Office for Publishing and Promotion Services, 1989), pp. 1-2; see also, Administrative Board, USCC, *The Many Faces of AIDS: A Gospel Response* (Washington, D.C.: USCC Office for Publishing and Promotion Services, 1987); The National Conference of Catholic Bishops and the United States Catholic Conference will continue to study questions related to the AIDS crisis, issuing other documents and updates as warranted.

and frustrations, or as the prey for the psychosexual disorders of others. Every girl and boy is entrusted to us—parents, family, friends, the Church, and the wider community—to be cared for, loved, educated, and fostered in the development of his or her fullest potential. No doubt parenting requires considerable commitment, patience, and understanding. The fact that some adults may not have the maturity or the skills to handle this responsibility well is no excuse for deliberate use and abuse of a child.

Likewise, professional care-givers, such as clergy, teachers, coaches, counselors, day-care personnel, baby-sitters, and medical professionals, are commissioned by parents or guardians and the community to assist in educating and helping young people grow and develop well. To abuse this trust by manipulating or preying upon young learners or clients for one's own sexual satisfaction is inexcusable and criminal behavior. Family members and institutions charged with hiring personnel to care for children, the elderly, and the mentally disabled, must also do so wisely, carefully screening and/or licensing those who will be entrusted with the care and/or education of these more vulnerable members of society.

Nor are children the only victims of sexual crimes and violent abuse. We unreservedly condemn the sexual abuse of spouses or social partners, most often women, by those who feel that sex is an absolute right and that one's partner is an outlet or object to be used. Since the Christian tradition teaches that sexual intercourse and conjugal love are designed by God to be symbols of total self-giving, intimacy, commitment, and fidelity, we reject any situation in which genital sex occurs as the result of manipulation, force, or coercion.

Children and adults who are the direct victims of physical, sexual, emotional, or verbal abuse deserve our compassion, care, professional help, and financial aid to escape such situations and to embark on a course of physical and psychological healing. Society, through its legal structures, law enforcement programs, and court systems, must stand firm against the sexual abuse and violent misuse of children, spouses, and other victims. The Church, likewise, strongly opposes any and all violations of human dignity and personal rights. We offer our various social service agencies and resources to help heal and/or rehabilitate the victims of sexual abuse and violence.

There is still, however, one more victim in the case of sexual abuse and violent misuse, whose dignity must be respected and whose needs must be met—the perpetrator, the abusive person himself or herself. Because past abuse by others or prior life experience and decisions often contribute to the reasons that sex offenders are who they are, in a number of cases, their personal moral responsibility is diminished or lacking. Abusive persons are in need of professional help to cope with their behavior patterns and the underlying pathology that prompts them. Visceral feeling of retribution in the wider community must be confronted and channeled into constructive programs for all the victims of such crimes, while still maintaining protection of society.

Finally, a word of encouragement for those men and women, boys and girls, who suffer from sexual problems. The pain of sexual dysfunction, the effects of sexual abuse, the consequences of sexually immature decisions, and other forms of sexually related hurt and harm can be discouraging, even alienating. Therefore, we urge all those affected not to lose faith in seeking a cure, recovery, or spiritual guidance. In all of these situations, we urge them to seek health in ways that enrich themselves as persons in the model of Jesus.

In Conclusion

This chapter has attempted to apply the values and principles outlined in previous chapters to specific vocations, life-styles, and situations. Such discernment and decision making call for a blend of Christian spirituality with the moral virtue of prudence or practical wisdom. In the final chapter, we will outline a framework for more formal sexuality education programs.

Chapter 5
Education in
Human Sexuality
Family, School, Church, and
Society in Partnership

Since parents have conferred life on their children, they have a most solemn obligation to educate their offspring. Hence, parents must be acknowledged as the first and foremost educators of their children. . . .

It is particularly in the Christian family . . . that from their earliest years children should be taught, according to the faith received in baptism, to have a knowledge of God, to worship Him, and to love their neighbor. Here, too, they gain their first experience of wholesome human companionship and of the Church. . . .

While belonging primarily to the family, the task of imparting education requires the help of society as a whole. In addition, therefore, to the rights of parents and of others to whom parents entrust a share in the work of education, certain rights and duties belong to the civil society. . . .

Finally, the office of educating belongs by a unique title to the Church . . . because she has the responsibility of announcing the way of salvation to all [people], of communicating the life of Christ to those who believe, and of assisting them with ceaseless concern so that they may grow into the fullness of that same life.[1]

We begin this chapter with a lengthy excerpt from the *Declaration on Christian Education,* promulgated a quarter of a century ago at the Second Vatican Council. The above quotation captures succinctly the layered or multileveled direction that is consonant with the responsible approach for education in human sexuality that we propose here. We believe that education in human sexuality is a cooperative venture, in which parents or guardians, as primary

---

1. *Declaration on Christian Education* (October 28, 1965), no. 3.

educators, are assisted by schools, the Church, and the wider society, focusing on the physical, psychological, moral, social, and spiritual development of each child or learner.

Parental Rights and Responsibilities
The Family Perspective

The bishops at Vatican II reflected a long-standing Catholic belief that since parents have conferred life on their children, they "have the original, primary and inalienable right to educate them." It is our fundamental conviction that in every rightly constituted society, parents or legal guardians "must be acknowledged as the first and foremost educators of their children."[2] However, this parental obligation and corresponding right is not grounded in some notion of property or possession, as if parents "own" or have "absolute control" over their children's lives and future destinies. Rather, the underlying basis for the parental obligation to educate their children is the absolute right of every child to "life, to bodily integrity, and to the means which are suitable for the proper development of life."[3] The procreative meaning of conjugal love has always included the responsibility not only to conceive and give birth to new life, but the correlative obligation to provide for the material and educational needs of children so conceived.

Responsible parenting involves the moral obligation to care for, nurture, and educate those children who are the fruit of a couple's two-in-one-flesh union.[4] As John Paul II phrases it:

> The task of giving education is rooted in the primary vocation of married couples to participate in God's creative activity: By begetting in love and for love a new person who has within himself or herself the vocation for growth and development, parents by that very fact take the task of helping that person effectively to live a fully human life.[5]

Every child deserves to be born into a loving, enriching family setting.

Life's beginning stages are of critical importance to individual growth and development. Here foundations are laid which influ-

2. Ibid.; *Charter of the Rights of the Family*, art. 5; *Decree on the Apostolate of the Laity*, no. 11; *Codex Iuris Canonici*, c. 793.
3. John XXIII, *Pacem in Terris* (April 11, 1963), no. 11.
4. Cf. *Codex Iuris Canonici*, c. 1055.1; *Pastoral Constitution on the Church in the Modern World*, no. 50.
5. *Familiaris Consortio*, no. 36.

ence the ability to accept self, relate to others, and respond effectively to the environment. Upon these foundations rests the formation of the basic human and Christian personality—and so also one's human capacity for relating to God.[6]

It is incumbent "on parents to create a family atmosphere so animated with love and reverence for God and others that a well-rounded personal and social development will be fostered among the children."[7] The family is thus the first environment of learning, in which children begin to learn the meaning of self-worth, of human dignity, of life, and of love.

It is appropriate that education in human sexuality find its primary locus within the family context. Each of us begins the long process of moving toward maturity from our first moments of life. Informal education in human sexuality begins right from birth. Particularly with regard to the sexuality education of young children, the family setting is the "preferential place," for parents seem best suited to offer "clear and delicate sex education" appropriately adapted to the age, maturity, and "sense of decency" of each child.[8] The Congregation for Catholic Education suggests that with regard to the more intimate aspects of sexuality, whether biological or affective, an individual education is desirable, preferably within the sphere of the family.[9]

Education in human sexuality in the home or family context is more "caught" than "taught," meaning that in the early years, it comes largely from participation and observation. "Christian parents must know that their example represents the most valid contribution in the education of their children."[10] What parents say, matters. And, if they match their words with corresponding actions, the message rings "loud and clear" that this is an important value for them, for this family, and for the young learner. So also, if parents fail to "practice what they preach," then the child receives a mixed message. Attitudes often speak louder than words.

Although parents or primary caretakers chart the general direction of family life and values, it is important to see each family as a more complex multifaceted system. Interaction with older or younger siblings, the presence or absence of grandparents, the degree of extended family relationships, ethnic homogeneity or

---

6. *Sharing the Light of Faith*, no. 177.
7. *Familiaris Consortio*, no. 36.
8. Cf. *Pastoral Constitution on the Church in the Modern World*, no. 49; *Educational Guidance in Human Love*, no. 15; *Familiaris Consortio*, no. 37.
9. See *Educational Guidance in Human Love*, no. 58.
10. Ibid., no. 15; see also nos. 48-55.

diversity, socioeconomic pressures, and subtle societal influences—all of these form part of the educational input that a child "absorbs" in his or her preschool years. While there is no perfect family, studies indicate that the more secure, loved, affirmed, accepted, and encouraged a child feels, the healthier and more productive his or her development will be. The family "is, in fact, the best environment to accomplish the obligation of securing a gradual education in sexual life. The family has an affective dignity which is suited to making acceptable without trauma the most delicate realities and to integrating them harmoniously in a balanced and rich personality."[11]

The family environment can be viewed as a relational testing ground. How male and female family members interact, their attitudes toward the worth of the child, and how they speak about and deal with genital functions, how they balance candor and modesty regarding sexual questions, all serve to "teach" children what it means to be human, to be male or female, and to be chaste. Providing clear information within the context of personal formation, geared to the age and maturity level of the child, requires grace and prudence on the part of parents, sisters and brothers, and other members of one's wider family.

Still, we cannot possibly isolate children from all of life's hurts or traumas. Part of the reality of maturing is learning to accept, to cope with, and, where possible, to rise above the effects of human frailty and sin. The Paschal Mystery involves both the harsh experience of crucifixion and pain as well as the glory of resurrection and new beginnings. Marital tension, sibling rivalry, illness, death, separation or divorce, socioeconomic limitations, and even, tragically, domestic violence and child abuse are some of the realities that children may experience in the course of growing up. Our intention here is not to accentuate the dark side of family life, but to highlight the fact that education for human living, including one's sexuality, begins long before the classroom and incorporates a variety of input. A child absorbs both our best intentions as well as our human foibles and sinful mistakes as material for his or her development and future decision making. While accentuating the call to be positive role models for children, we are mindful that real families make mistakes.

We join other church and community leaders and educators in calling parents, guardians, and all family members to accept the

---

11. Ibid., no. 48.

challenge of being good teachers to the young and to one another, modeling basic human and Christian virtues—love, respect for self/others, commitment, honesty, patience, self-control, forgiveness, and prudence. Christian family life is the first experience of the Church for young children. "The Christian family constitutes a specific revelation and realization of ecclesial communion, and for this reason, too, it can and should be called 'the domestic church.'"[12] Parents, children, and extended family members are called to make the Church real for one another, to be, in miniature, the Body of Christ.

We pledge ourselves and our institutions to support individuals, couples, and all families, particularly those with special needs. By virtue of the sacraments of baptism, confirmation, and Eucharist, the child is initiated into the community of the faithful. The community pledges its support to walk with this child on the faith journey. At the same time, the Church acts to support parents in their role as the first and foremost educators. The Word of God, the sacraments, and the power of prayer are readily available to help nourish and heal individuals and families along the way. So also, Catholic parishes, parochial schools, religious education programs, and the varied services and programs of Catholic Charities exist to assist people in being healthy, whole, holy, and productive.

Education in Human Sexuality
Parents, Schools, Religious Education, and Church as Partners

Each child is a mysterious gift from God, entrusted not only to one's parents, but to the whole community as well. One's wider family, the church community, and the society at large, all have an interest in protecting new members, in safeguarding their rights and fostering their growth and development. Also, what parents say and practice at home needs to be reaffirmed and reinforced by the wider community. Therefore, John Paul II has noted that "[t]he family is the primary but not the only and exclusive educating community."[13]

Some parents feel uneasy, at times incapable of serving as sexuality educators for their own children, particularly in content areas

---

12. *Familiaris Consortio*, no. 21; see also nos. 39, 49, 55; *Dogmatic Constitution on the Church*, no. 11.
13. *Familiaris Consortio*, no. 40.

that require a more sophisticated understanding of biology and the human sciences. Other parents, because of their own insecurities or personal problems, feel unable to do justice to their children in certain educational fields like sexuality. "If parents do not feel able to perform this duty, they may have recourse to others who enjoy their confidence."[14] The wider community, both civil and ecclesial, has a cooperative role to play in meeting the educational needs of these children of God, members of the human family.[15]

Various civil and church agents and programs of education "are necessary, even though each can and should play its part in accordance with the special competence and contribution proper to itself."[16] Parochial and public school systems should supplement and enhance parental educational efforts, never override or countermand them, except in those exceptional situations where parental neglect or child abuse occur. Barring such abuse, John Paul II affirms that the "right of parents to choose an education in conformity with their religious faith must be absolutely guaranteed."[17] He goes on to say that "corresponding to their right, parents have a serious duty to commit themselves totally to a cordial and active relationship with the teachers and school authorities."[18]

We applaud the generally favorable partnerships that exist in this country between parishioners and Catholic schools and among the wider society and public school boards and administrators. We believe that "close cooperation with the family is especially important when treating sensitive issues such as religious, moral, or sexual education; orientation toward a profession; or a choice of one's vocation in life."[19] We affirm the value of well-planned instruction in human sexuality for all people, especially for children and adolescents. Whether done in the family setting or in carefully planned school or religious education programs, such instruction always should be adapted to the age, background, and maturity level of the learners involved.

In a Catholic context, the purpose of such education in human sexuality, whether formal or informal, is threefold:

1. To give each learner an understanding of the nature and importance of sexuality as a divine gift, a fundamental component of

14. *Educational Guidance in Human Love*, no. 59.
15. Cf. *Educational Guidance in Human Love*, nos. 51, 53, 64; *Declaration on Christian Education*, no. 3.
16. *Familiaris Consortio*, no. 14.
17. Ibid., no. 40, also no. 46; *Codex Iuris Canonici*, c. 793; *Charter of the Rights of the Family*, art. 5.
18. Ibid., no. 40.
19. Congregation for Catholic Education, *The Religious Dimension of Education in a Catholic School* (April 7, 1988), no. 42; *Educational Guidance in Human Love*, no. 54.

personality, and an enrichment of the whole person—body, emotions, soul—whose deepest meaning is to lead the person to the gift of self in love.[20]

2. To give each learner an appreciation of chastity as a virtue that develops a person's authentic maturity and makes him or her capable of guiding the sexual instinct in the service of love and integrating it into his or her psychological and spiritual development.[21]

3. To give each learner an appreciation of the human and Christian values that sexuality is intended to express and to lead each learner to a knowledge of, respect for, and sincere personal adherence to the moral norms regarding sexuality that are taught by the Church.[22]

Sexuality education is not reducible to a set of simple teaching materials about human organ systems and their biological functions. Nor can it be taught in one isolated course or in the abstract realm of theory alone. The ultimate objective of education in human sexuality is the personal realization of total sexual identity and the affective maturation of the learner. This includes not only mastering data related to one's sexual organs, hormones, and bodily functions, but also acquiring a more mature perception concerning oneself, interpersonal relationships, and the human and Christian values at stake. Over time, the learner will develop a sense of self-control appropriate to his or her vocation in life and mature in understanding sexual morality in accord with the Church's teaching and tradition.[23] Such understanding will enable each learner to realize that the constant struggle to live in accord with the Christian vision of sexuality is sustained by divine grace, through the Word of God received in faith, through prayer, and through participation in the sacraments. Information about sexual functions and human reproduction is inextricably linked to formation in human values and Christian morality.

Education in human sexuality in a public school setting, where no sectarian religious value system is taught, will be more difficult. Regrettably, in our country today, the dominant interpretation of the separation of church and state precludes any discussion of religious values. However, "without teaching the beliefs of any one religious group, the public schools must nonetheless ensure that

---

20. Cf. *Educational Guidance in Human Love,* nos. 4, 16; *Familiaris Consortio,* nos. 37, 11, 32.
21. Cf. *Educational Guidance,* nos. 4, 18, 34; *Familiaris Consortio,* no. 37.
22. Cf. *Educational Guidance,* nos. 19, 40; *Familiaris Consortio,* nos. 33, 37.
23. See *Educational Guidance,* no. 70.

fundamental human and moral values form an integral part of their programs."[24]

We welcome the renewed emphasis, in recent years, on values education in public schools. In many areas, public schools have become a major purveyor of human values, while home, church, and local community, regrettably, have taken a lesser role. Especially where this has happened, it is imperative that basic human values be respected, taught, and promoted. No school setting is values-free. No educational experience is values-free—all the more reason, then, for parents to be involved in the development of curriculum and school policies and programs. Also, it is imperative that public educational enterprises respect the rightful place of religious beliefs and values in the families they serve. Parents, on their part, must ensure that a proper respect is accorded their own religious beliefs and perspectives. Parents need to be made aware of their rights and responsibilities in this regard.

Diocesan leaders are encouraged to assist parents whose children are enrolled in school to become actively involved in the formation, implementation, and evaluation of programs of education in human sexuality. Exercising their role as parents, they need the support and assistance of the Church as they work to ensure that schools respect the values of the family and their faith tradition.

In order to ensure the development and acceptance of a program of sexuality instruction that meets the needs of the learners as well as the concerns of parents and professional educators, three rules must be scrupulously observed in the planning process, whether in a parochial or a public education setting:

1. Begin with parental involvement.

2. Include parents throughout the planning and execution phases of the program.

3. Have parents integrally involved in the evaluation process after the program is complete.

To enhance the possibility for a successful program and to merit general community support, any program in human sexuality must be planned carefully. It is better to move cautiously and to consider the needs and sensitivities of all involved. Initial planning committees should include representatives of the parents of chil-

---

24. *A Joint Pastoral Statement on Education in Human Sexuality*, no. 13.

dren to be involved in the program as well as educational professionals and experts from the fields of medicine, religion, ethics, psychology, and counseling. Open lines of communication from the beginning as well as a free exchange of information and proposed classroom materials will go a long way toward establishing parental support, while dispelling rumors and inordinate fears. Prudence dictates that parents and school authorities consider the implication and mode of presenting specific aspects of education in sexuality to a mixed audience of boys and girls. Only a strict collaboration between the school and the family will be able to guarantee an advantageous exchange of experience between parents and teachers for the good of the learners involved.

If the Catholic school or religious education program proposes one set of values, which are countermanded either by word or unreflected deed at home, the student will be more confused than helped. That is why we wholeheartedly support what is called a *family perspective* when doing education in human sexuality.[25] Viewing each student in the context of his or her distinct family configuration and network of other social relationships acknowledges that when one person "learns" new material or behaviors or values, that change will have a ripple effect—for good or ill—on people around them, young and old alike. Since actions often speak louder than words, the power of parental or family example in living the Christian life should not be underestimated.

Therefore, we recommend that parents, other adult family members, and other siblings be included in the learning process by involvement in the execution of the program, ideally through simultaneous or parallel sessions aimed at their own maturity levels and personal needs. "A solid catechetical preparation of adults on human love establishes the foundations for the sex[uality] education of children. Thus the possession of human maturity illumined by faith is secured, which will be decisive in the dialogue which adults are called to establish with the new generations."[26]

However, we also propose that religious and sexuality educators need to give more attention to programs aimed at the personal needs of adults, for their own sake.

It should not be thought that adult catechesis is important only by reason of its relationship to the catechesis of children. . . . Rather, the

25. See *A Family Perspective in Church and Society*. This practical and helpful document focuses on education recipients as interpersonal beings, living in family networks, rather than as isolated consumers.
26. *Educational Guidance in Human Love*, no. 63.

primary reason for adult catechesis—its first and essential objective—is to help adults themselves grow to maturity of faith as members of the Church and society.[27]

As we have noted throughout this document, one's growth in understanding human sexuality does not end with puberty or marriage or some threshold thereafter. We remain sexual beings from the moment of conception to the grave. Sexual feelings and the need to relate such feelings to the Christian call to love and to be loved remain with us throughout life. Education in human sexuality is thus a lifelong process, a developmental learning experience that ripens, evolves, and, it is hoped, matures across the years and the decades.[28] We encourage ongoing formation in human sexuality not only for children and adolescents but for all people, particularly at key junctures in life (e.g., puberty, engagement/marriage, parenthood, divorce or widowhood, ordination, religious vows). The various vocational groups discussed in the previous chapter have distinct sexual needs and issues, which might be dealt with best in sexuality education forums focused on each.

Parental Approval, Discretion, and Limits

Sex[uality] education, which is a basic right and duty of parents, must always be carried out under their attentive guidance, whether at home or in education centers chosen and controlled by them. In this regard, the Church affirms the law of subsidiarity, which the school is bound to observe when it cooperates in sex[uality] education, by entering into the same spirit that animates the parents.[29]

Having affirmed that parents have a right and a responsibility to be involved in the development of formal sexuality programs designed to meet the educational needs of their children, we hasten to add that such programs, once prepared, ought not to be imposed automatically upon all families. As noted earlier, the Congregation for Catholic Education suggests that catechesis in human sexuality done in the family context "constitutes a privileged form, . . . the preferential place for education of young people in chastity."[30] Therefore, parents or guardians who wish to withhold permission

---

27. *Sharing the Light of Faith*, no. 40.
28. Cf. *Educational Guidance in Human Love*, no. 41; *To Teach as Jesus Did*, no. 43.
29. *Familiaris Consortio*, no. 37.
30. *Educational Guidance in Human Love*, nos. 15, 59; see also nos. 48, 58.

for their children, especially the very young, to participate in formal sexuality education programs outside the home ought to be respected. However, they are to be encouraged strongly to offer comparable sexuality education within the family setting.

However, the sincere willingness of some parents to offer such "in home" instruction is not necessarily synonymous with their ability to do so. The Church can be of great help in assisting parents to be better sexuality educators in the family context. Appropriate reading materials and audiovisuals, borrowed or purchased from Catholic catechetical centers or bookstores, can be used by parents in instructing their children. Adult sexuality catechesis should help parents to be more competent and at ease with respect to sexual content and teaching methods.[31]

Still, the Congregation for Catholic Education notes:

> The difficulties which sex[uality] education often encounters within the bosom of the family solicit a major commitment on the part of the Christian community and, in particular, of priests to collaborate in the education of the baptized. In this field, the Catholic school, the parish and other ecclesial institutions are called to collaborate with the family.[32]

As highlighted in the lengthy quotation at the beginning of this chapter, the Church shares a co-responsibility with the parents to ensure that each child is educated properly in the truths of the Catholic tradition, including those related to one's sexuality: personal worth, human dignity and equality, respect for life, honesty, fairness, chaste living, responsible parenthood, and sexual moral norms.[33]

In *Sharing the Light of Faith: The National Catechetical Directory for Catholics of the United States*, we attempted to delineate more clearly this balance of rightful parental discretion with the correlative responsibility we share as official teachers and pastors in the Church:

> Parents have a right and duty to protest programs which violate their moral and religious convictions. If protests based on well-founded convictions and accurate information are unsuccessful, they have a right to remove their children from the classes, taking care to cause as little embarrassment to the children as possible.[34]

---

31. See *Sharing the Light of Faith*, no. 191.
32. *Educational Guidance in Human Love*, no. 54.
33. Cf. ibid., nos. 55, 53; *Declaration on Christian Education*, no. 3.
34. *Sharing the Light of Faith*, no. 191; see similar ideas in *To Teach as Jesus Did*, no. 57; *Declaration on Christian Education*, no. 1.

The document goes on to speak to those parents who may be opposed categorically to all formal instruction in human sexuality:

> Even after their reasonable requirements and specifications have been met, however, some parents may remain anxious about education in sexuality. They should not let their feelings express themselves in indiscriminate opposition to all classroom instruction in sexuality, for that would not be consistent with the position of the Second Vatican Council and the bishops of the United States.[35]

The document cautions these parents not to overstate their personal objections, lest the rights of equally sincere and responsible parents and the responsibility of competent church leaders to assist them be infringed upon:

> Furthermore, to the extent such opposition might impede or disrupt responsible efforts along these lines, it would violate the rights of other, no less conscientious, parents who desire such instruction for their children.[36]

We acknowledge the diversity of opinion in the Catholic community in this country as to the value of formal instruction in human sexuality in general. We are aware of the subsequent controversies surrounding the particular content or set of fundamental principles to be taught in specific programs.

However, we believe that the guidelines in *Sharing the Light of Faith* (quoted above) as well as those in *Educational Guidance in Human Love* affirm the right of parents, educational professionals, and church leaders cooperatively to implement formal instruction programs that are responsible, morally sound, in accord with official Catholic teaching, and sufficiently "clear and delicate" for the learning audiences targeted. We also respect the right of parents with school-aged children to be the final arbitrators of what sort of program best meets the needs of their particular child for education in human sexuality.

The Teaching Profession
A Noble Calling

Before concluding this chapter, we wish to speak briefly about the challenging vocation of all those who assist parents in fulfilling their educational responsibility, and who represent the wider

---

35. Ibid.
36. Ibid.

Church and society as well, by undertaking the demanding role of teacher in a parochial school or religious education program. "This calling requires extraordinary qualities of mind and heart, extremely careful preparation, and a constant readiness to begin anew and to adapt."[37] All the more so, those men and women who are entrusted with the responsibility of teaching human sexuality, especially to children, must be gifted individuals, carefully chosen and well prepared for the task.

Teachers of sexuality education must realize the great trust that parents, the Church, and the society are placing in them. The personality, professional training, and psychological balance of a teacher strongly influence one's students. A competent teacher of human sexuality, therefore, must have a complete and accurate theoretical knowledge of the meaning and value of sexuality and, at the same time, be personally mature, integrated, and responsible in his or her own sexual identity.[38]

"The teacher who carries out his or her task outside the family context needs a suitable and serious psychopedagogical training which allows the seizing of particular situations which require a special solicitude."[39] A gradual or evolutionary approach to the subject is warranted, attentive to the stages of physical and psychological maturity of the individual learners. The teacher must respect the privacy of the learner and treat the learner's personal sharing with confidentiality. A good teacher must be able to discern when learners have assimilated particular values, are motivated properly, and comprehend the causes, connections, and purposes for proposed courses of behavior.[40] At the same time, long-range planning, adequate teacher and parent training, and effective educational materials will all contribute to a more effective program. It is also important to build periodic updates and ongoing professional support into the training process for sexuality educators themselves as well as for their team or faculty colleagues.

Underneath or behind it all stands the person of the teacher himself or herself. The selection of individuals to implement sexuality instruction programs ought to be done carefully. Not everyone who is a competent teacher or catechist will be an effective sexuality educator. One should look for persons of faith who are willing as well as competent. They should be people who possess

---

37. *Declaration on Christian Education*, no. 5.
38. See *Educational Guidance in Human Love*, no. 79.
39. Ibid., no. 81.
40. See ibid., no. 85.

and demonstrate moral maturity; who seem to be sexually integrated and at peace with themselves; and who are at ease discussing, in a clear and delicate manner, such topics as intimacy, sexuality, love, moral values, chastity, and the reproductive system. In all of this, a proper understanding of and fidelity to the Church's teachings is an essential quality for those who teach in these programs.

Objectivity and *prudence* are two characteristics singled out by the Congregation for Catholic Education as earmarks of good teaching. Teachers of human sexuality must not be reticent to speak candidly and objectively about sexual matters. Sensitivity to age and a respect for individual differences among learners require that teachers sometimes give partial explanations, but always according to the truth. Prudence, the virtue of practical wisdom, allows an effective teacher to adapt material to the needs of a given learner, to choose language carefully, as well as to select the right time and teaching method to be employed.[41] As we mentioned in reference to parents as educators, all effective teachers demonstrate, by word and action, that they believe the values concerning sexuality that they teach.

Personal integrity or *authenticity* is the ultimate characteristic of the good teacher, whether one is a professional educator or volunteer in a formal setting or a conscientious parent in the family setting. A good educator is also a good listener, a person who allows the learner to ask questions, clarify and pursue personal concerns, all in the hope that insight and deeper understanding will follow.

We commend those teachers already involved in sexuality education and those contemplating such a vocation. We pray for them and invite their further involvement in and reliance on the church community for personal enrichment, for spiritual nourishment, for ethical content, and for moral support. Their profession is indeed a "vocation," a divine calling to serve by modeling and articulating what it means to be a mature sexual person—gifted and growing in the ability to love and be loved, chaste in one's particular vocation or life-style, and responsible for one's moral choices and actions, all in the light of church teaching.

---

41. See ibid., no. 87.

Epilogue

Like the mission and message of Jesus Christ, the Church's educational mission, including education in human sexuality, is universal—for all people, at all times, in all places.[1] As Christians, members of the Catholic Church, we are called to a "continuous, permanent conversion."[2] As individual sojourners and as a pilgrim community we are called to consider, judge, and arrange our lives according to the holiness and love of God.[3]

> God signifies an alternative impulse—to sacrifice rather than grab, to love rather than lust, to give rather than take, to pursue truth rather than promote lies, to humble oneself rather than inflate the ego. In all creation, the hand of God is seen; in every human heart; in a blade of grass as in great trees and mountains and rivers; in the first stirring of life in a fetus and in the last musings and mutterings of a tired mind.[4]

The mission to provide education and lifelong learning for ourselves and our children concerning human sexuality is not exhausted by any single program, institution, or approach. By their complementary and cooperative efforts, individuals, parents, families, schools, churches, and the wider society can work together to educate all people about this gift called sexuality. We believe that blending moral and values-based *formation* with clear and factual *information* is the best approach to sexuality education, whether done in the family setting or in more formal programs or some combination of the two.

This pastoral document is not the last word on the subject of human sexuality, but we believe it is an important word. We have presented a positive and hopeful Christian vision of what it means to be sexual and to be chaste. As we close this reflection on the mystery and challenge of responsible acceptance of the great gift of human sexuality, we echo once again the themes of chapter one, which grounded the entire enterprise:

---

1. Cf. *To Teach as Jesus Did*, no. 154.
2. *Familiaris Consortio*, no. 9.
3. Cf. *Paenitemini*.
4. Malcolm Muggeridge, *Confessions of a Twentieth-Century Pilgrim* (San Francisco: Harper & Row, 1988), p. 67.

83

- Human sexuality is a precious gift from God. All of us must approach the topic with a deep and abiding sense of appreciation, wonder, and respect.

- Each of us is entrusted by God with the awesome responsibility to guide and direct this gift wisely and lovingly.

- The incarnation and redemptive life, death, resurrection, and promised return of Jesus Christ make available the inspiration and grace to respond more fully to God's call to be chaste, to live sexually responsible lives.

Appendix

A Framework of Education in Human Sexuality: Some Principles and Recommendations

Preamble

This document from the U.S. bishops, *Human Sexuality: A Catholic Perspective for Education and Lifelong Learning,* provides clear guidance for those responsible for education and lifelong learning opportunities in the Catholic community. The following guidelines outline basic principles from this document and make particular recommendations for educating about human sexuality at five stages of human development. Diocesan leaders can use these guidelines for in-service workshops, organizing curricula, or talking with parents and others about educating Catholics in human sexuality.

Our growth in understanding human sexuality does not end with puberty or marriage or some subsequent threshold in life. Ongoing formation in human sexuality is for all people—young or old, married or single, disabled or able-bodied, ordained or those with religious vows.

The ultimate goal of education in human sexuality is a personal realization of sexual identity, as well as spiritual, moral, and affective maturation. This includes acquiring a holistic perception concerning self, interpersonal relationships, and the human and Christian values involved, as well as mastering data related to human anatomy and physiology. The Scriptures, Christian tradition, and the authentic teaching office of the Church help form our Catholic perspective. This blending of moral and values-based formation with clear and factual information is the best approach to sexuality education.

Parents have a most solemn obligation to educate their offspring, including matters of sexuality. They are assisted in this task by educators working in schools, parishes, and dioceses. It is vital that educators involve parents in the planning, programming, and implementation of formal human-sexuality education programs. Educators work not only with children but also with other adults, who continue to grow in their understanding of sexuality.

It is our intention that family life specialists, sexuality educators, and diocesan leaders, in reading the general principles and educational guidelines that follow, will develop appropriate perspectives to meet the specific needs of individuals, families, and communities. It is also important to note that the general principles apply to *every* stage of development and need to be incorporated in planning. Educators should take into account the age and maturity of the learners. In addition, diocesan leaders need to continue to build on guidelines from previous stages, since they are developmental, not isolated!

Because diocesan leaders need to address a variety of people and situations, here are some areas of special concern that are applicable across the spectrum of ages and developmental stages:

Cultural and Ethnic Diversity

In light of American pluralism and regional realities, leaders need to assess the people with whom they work. Values and culture are intertwined, so both must be reflected in developing programs and policies. A person's culture must be respected as well as examined in the light of human values and church teaching. Within a culture, there are various ethnic groups. While there may be a common language and faith, persons may come from different countries with varying dialects, attitudes, values, traditions, and histories. Diocesan leaders need to take into consideration the unique heritage of participants.

Regional Adaptations

It is also important to note regional differences, whether urban, suburban, rural, or various locales within the United States. Customs, vocabulary, and attitudes may differ. Sensitivity to regional needs is essential in developing policies, programs, and services.

Respect for Persons

Every human person has a distinct worth and dignity. Recognition of the value of each person is reflected in the ways in which people relate to each other, whether persons of the same or opposite gender. The skills for honest communication, for listening to others, for sharing, forgiving, and trusting are important elements for continual formation. There is need to affirm the equality and mutuality of men and women in attitudes, language, and behavior. Parents and educators have a unique privilege and responsibility in helping young people to learn this respect and to deepen their awareness of the dignity of others.

Persons with Disabilities

All persons are sexual beings. Persons may have a mental handicap or be physically disabled, but their sexual development is similar to others in their life stage. These principles and guidelines apply to persons who are disabled. Some persons may need special pastoral care or education. For example, when designing policies or programs, leaders need to consider the mental age and life experience of those who are mentally handicapped. Special care needs to be provided for individual cases.

Family Diversity

Families take many forms and configurations today: nuclear, extended, single or multiple generations, two-parent, single-parent, single-earner, dual-earner, dual-career, childless, blended, divorced and separated families. It is important for diocesan leaders to address various family models in services rendered.

Maturity

Participants in sexuality education programs may be more or less mature within a given developmental stage. In the early adolescent and adolescent stages, females generally mature more quickly, both physically and emotionally. When teaching children the informational side of human sexuality, the degree of maturity more than the chronological age should determine the content to be offered. Leaders, then, need to adapt guidelines according to the degree of personal and sexual maturity.

Sensitivity to Problems

Parents and teachers involved in sexuality education at times will hear questions and observe behaviors in children and youth that are of concern to them. Sexual abuse, psychosexual maldevelopment, even psychiatric illness may appear. In such situations parents and teachers are encouraged to consult with each other and to take necessary actions to protect the child. Besides conforming to local laws, parents and teachers may need to seek competent legal and psychological help for the appropriate parties and to ensure any other action for the personal welfare of all involved.

Pastoral and mental health professionals can be very useful at these times. The more familiar parents and teachers are with psychosexual problems that may impact children and youth, the more they will be able to help. Diocesan leaders need to assist in this most important work.

Overview

Two main sections follow: *General Principles* and *Guidelines for Developmental Stages.*

The *General Principles* apply to all persons engaged in human sexuality education, both teachers and learners. These fundamental ideas should be taught and learned early in life and guide our sexuality as long as we live. They are underlying assumptions about who we are and how we live out our sexuality and must be integrated with the specific principles at each developmental stage. (The chapter references in parentheses refer to *Human Sexuality: A Catholic Perspective for Education and Lifelong Learning.*)

The *Guidelines for Developmental Stages* present the characteristics and guidelines applicable to each life stage. No stage stands on its own. Each builds on what has happened in the previous stage and prepares people for the next. The same is true for the educational guidelines. They stand in concert with guidelines preceding and following them, as well as with the *General Principles.*

General Principles

Precious Gift (Chapter 1)

- Human sexuality is a divine gift, a blend of spirit and body that shares in God's creative love and life.

- We approach human sexuality with a deep and abiding sense of appreciation, wonder, and respect.

- The divine becoming human adds greater dignity to our being embodied, sexual beings. Through Jesus' birth, life, death, resurrection, and promised return, we can become our best selves, able with God's help to overcome temptation of any kind.

Body (Chapter 3)

- The human body is good. We are enfleshed sexual beings, male and female.

- In our efforts to love, we make real and incarnate God's goodness, love, and vitality.

- Respect for the human body is reflected in how we care for ourselves physically, emotionally, and spiritually.

Love (Chapter 2)

- Created in God's likeness, we are called to a life of loving and being loved. Love is the basic vocation we all share. We begin with love, continue in love, and reach our fulfillment of love through, with, and in God when we die.

- The desire to be loved and to love, to be united with one another, is a deep-seated and natural yearning.

- Love involves personal decision characterized by commitment, self-sacrifice and perseverance.

- Our sexuality, as distinct from sexual activity, is an innate force that can draw us out of ourselves into loving relationships.

Sin (Chapter 1)

- While we are called to incarnate the image of God in the way we live and love, the gift of human sexuality also can be abused, sometimes intentionally, sometimes through immaturity or ignorance.

- Temptations to subvert our human desires, including sexual ones, into purely selfish aims or to manipulate others in human relationships have been experienced in our hearts and in human history.

Forgiveness (Chapter 2)

- We are aware of our own frailty and sin as well as God's abiding presence and promise of forgiveness.

- As members of the Church, we draw strength, comfort, and renewed challenge from the Word of God, the Eucharist, and the healing and strengthening power of the sacrament of reconciliation.

Call to Holiness (Chapter 2)

- There is a universal calling in every human heart to be personally whole and spiritually holy.

- Dealing creatively with one's own sexuality—gender, sexual feelings, desires—is a fundamental challenge in every person's quest for maturity and holiness.

- Spirituality, rightly understood, implies a lifelong process of conversion. In both, we look at our lives in the light of God's love, try to live out the death-resurrection-present reign of Jesus in everyday circumstances, and change those things that isolate and alienate us from God, self, and one another.

Formation/Information (Chapter 2)

- Blending moral and values-based *formation* with clear and factual *information* is the best approach to sexuality education, whether done in the family setting or in more formal programs or in some combination of the two.

Education/Conscience (Chapter 2)

- Educators in human sexuality must both teach and listen. They need to be able to convey the Church's teachings with authority, candor, sound reasoning, fidelity, and a sensitivity to the age and maturity level of their audience. They must also take time to listen to questions, concerns and insights; to respect learners' integrity and sincerity; and to facilitate their ongoing conscience formation.

- Each person has an obligation to form a correct conscience. It is the responsibility of Catholic educators to assist them in the process by articulating church teaching in its entirety and in its integrity.

Moral Decision Making (Chapter 2)

- The Church believes there are objectively right and wrong answers to moral dilemmas. The process of moving from absolute values to general norms to specific case judgments requires the virtue of prudence, the ability to exercise sound judgment in practical matters.

- Discernment of moral choices involves the formation of a correct conscience by a process of using one's reasoning ability, the sources of divine revelation (Scripture and tradition), the Church's teaching and guidance, the wise counsel of others, and one's own individual and communal experience of prayer and grace.

Roles and Responsibilities (Chapter 5)

- Parents and the family comprise the first and most important context for sharing faith, forming attitudes, fostering values, and sharing information. Children have a right to life, education, bodily integrity, and the means for holistic human development.

- The role of the Church in human sexuality education is one of both teacher and healer.

- Professional educators assist parents in fulfilling their educational responsibilities. They represent the wider Church and society. The profession of educating in human sexuality is a call to model and articulate what it means to be a mature sexual person.

- Education in human sexuality is a cooperative venture among parents, schools, Church, and the wider society.

Personal Responsibility (Chapter 1)

- Each of us is entrusted by God with the awesome responsibility to guide and direct our gift of sexuality wisely and lovingly.

- At best, our sexuality calls us to personal maturity and interpersonal commitments.

Sexuality and Sex (Chapter 1)

- Sexuality refers to a fundamental component of personality in and through which we, as male or female, experience our relatedness to self, others, the world, and even God.

- Sex refers *either* to the biological aspects of being male or female (i.e., synonym for one's gender) *or* to the expressions of sexuality, which have physical, emotional, social, and spiritual dimensions.

Sexual Beings (Chapters 1, 3)

- We are sexual beings from conception to death.

Equality of Male and Female (Chapters 1, 3)

- Both man and woman are persons—equal yet distinct.

- Man and woman share a basic mutuality.

Chastity (Chapters 2, 3, 4)

- Every person is a sexual being, called to be chaste, that is, to do what is sexually responsible for one's state in life.

- Chastity consists in guiding the sexual instinct to the service of love and of integrating it in the development of the person.

Genital Sexual Intimacy (Chapters 3, 4)

- The gift of the body in sexual intercourse is a real symbol of the giving of the whole person.

- The Church's teaching on genital sex is rooted in a profound respect for the dignity and uniqueness of human persons.

- Genital sexual union has its true meaning and moral integrity only in the context of marriage.

- Outside the context of marriage, genital sexual intimacy, however well intended, is not an expression of *total* self-giving. Objectively speaking, it is morally wrong.

Marriage (Chapters 2, 3, 4)

- Marriage is both a unitive and procreative community of love, bound by an unbreakable pledge of fidelity, a covenant that is deeper than any civil contract.

- Christian marriage is a sacrament by which man and woman profess to each other solemn vows of love and fidelity, which serve as the outward sign of an interior reality.

- Marriage is a lifelong sacrament. The ongoing growth in understanding and living the sacramentality of marriage begins with remote and immediate preparation for marriage and continues with support throughout the years of married life.

Single Life (Chapter 4)

- The single way of life represents a wide variety of life-styles in our culture: temporarily or permanently single, divorced, separated, and widowed.

- Mature, single persons, seek a careful balance between a healthy independence, with a reasonable degree of privacy and freedom, and the need for love, including genuine intimacy and community belonging.

Celibacy (Chapter 4)

- Celibacy accepted for the sake of the reign of God serves as a complement to the vocation of marriage.

- Celibates choose not to give their life to any one person and are challenged to share it generously with many people.

- Sexuality is a dynamic element in the life of ordained, vowed, and promised celibates.

Early Childhood

In the beginning years of life (birth to six years), children grow rapidly in many ways. There are physical, cognitive, affective, social, and spiritual developments. Infants and toddlers evidence certain characteristics, which are then further developed in the later years of this stage and which contribute to their understanding of human sexuality.

Characteristics of Young Children

Infants and toddlers discover the body through looking and touching and grow in their ability to control bodily functions. Through word and gesture, music, dance, and role playing, they learn to express themselves. Their natural curiosity and imagination motivate their cognitive learning as well as their spiritual development.

As they progress through the later stage of early childhood, children achieve more independence in caring for their bodies. As they begin to accept themselves as unique persons, children also come to a clearer understanding of their identity as boys or girls. Their ability to ask questions, make choices, know right from wrong, and accept responsibility for their actions is evident in their behavior. Spiritually, children begin to pray formally and spontaneously, trusting in God, who loves and cares for them.

In the early childhood stage, it is important for children to have around them significant adults for purposes of bonding, nurturing, and guiding. Parents/guardians provide a sense of security for their children and help their sons and daughters to accept themselves without guilt or shame.

Socially, young children begin to move from total self-centeredness to a limited sense of others. They begin the process of socialization through interaction with siblings, friends, and significant adults. Children's ability to share and also to experience and express forgiveness is learned best from adults and from relationships with their peers.

Guidelines for Early Childhood

The following guidelines apply when educating young children about human sexuality. They are to be used in conjunction with Human Sexuality: A Catholic Perspective for Education and Lifelong Learning *and with the* General Principles *that are included in this*

Appendix. These General Principles *apply to all stages of development. It is helpful to remember that one stage builds on another, and that stages of growth and development often overlap.*

Because each child has the right to life, bodily integrity, and the means for proper development, educators need to help parents/guardians understand the physical, cognitive, affective, social, and spiritual development of young children. Some areas to address include:

- providing a wholesome and safe environment;

- conveying to children that they are loved, valued, cherished, and prized;

- providing first experiences of God's love communicated through the love of family members for one another and for them; and

- helping children develop a personal relationship with God, especially through prayer.

Because the body is a sacred gift, educators in human sexuality need to encourage parents/guardians in helping children to be comfortable with their bodies. Some areas to address include:

- giving children proper names for body parts;

- instructing children to respect and care for their own bodies, including hygiene, good eating habits, and exercise;

- educating children to respect others' bodies; and

- teaching the difference between appropriate touch and inappropriate touch.

Because children at this age are naturally curious about their bodies and the bodies of others, educators need to assist parents/guardians in affirming the goodness of their children's bodies. Some areas to address include:

- understanding the naturalness of children's actions, especially regarding elimination and knowledge of sexual parts; and

- accepting children's actions that are natural, while assisting them to know what is appropriate behavior.

Because young children are highly impressionable, educators need to assist parents/guardians in creating a wholesome environment that will foster children's growth and development in human sexuality. Some areas to address include:

- moderating and supervising television programs and print materials;

- being alert to nonverbal communication as well as direct questions;

- being discreet regarding their own sexual behavior; and

- being selective in choosing care-givers.

Because building self-esteem begins at birth and is a foundation for all levels of development, educators need to enable parents/guardians to recognize and respect the uniqueness of each child. Some areas to address include:

- enabling children to accept themselves as total persons, with strengths and limitations, as God created them;

- helping children to distinguish between persons who by nature are good and behavior that may be undesirable; and

- respecting the dignity of children verbally, physically, and emotionally.

Because children at this stage develop trust by relating with significant adults, educators need to encourage parents/guardians to be open, honest, available, and caring. Some areas to address include:

- answering questions honestly, correctly, and with language children can understand;

- giving parental warmth and affection, especially through the sense of touch;

- spending significant time with each child; and

- providing opportunities for children to interact with adults outside the home.

Because children learn through observation and experience, educators need to encourage parents/guardians to be role models. Some areas to address include:

- providing opportunities for children to witness loving relationships;

- having children experience single persons and celibate persons as loving beings; and

- giving appropriate, clear answers to questions about lifestyles.

Because making choices is the basis for moral decision making and the formation of conscience, educators need to support parents/ guardians as they provide situations that ask for choices. Some areas to address include:

- allowing children to make simple choices that will develop a pattern of making free decisions;

- giving gentle, ongoing guidance on what is morally good;

- helping children learn the consequences of actions;

- providing a healthy balance of both structured and free play; and

- helping children distinguish between safe and dangerous situations.

Because children of this age are curious about the differences between boys/men and girls/women, educators need to encourage parents/guardians in affirming the equality of men and women in word, attitude, and action. Some areas to address include:

- creating an atmosphere that includes loving modeling by adults;

- fostering appropriate use of inclusive language;

- appreciating the equality and mutuality of men and women;

- exploring gender roles regarding work and family;

- providing a variety of role models;

- allowing children to discover various ways to play and interact; and

- accepting children without stereotyped role and gender expectations.

For further development of the issues identified in these guidelines, refer to the text of the foundational document.

Childhood

This developmental stage builds on early childhood. Some of the characteristics will overlap, as will some of the guidelines. Children in this stage of development will possess varying degrees of maturity and of readiness for education in human sexuality. Educators need to make adaptations accordingly.

Characteristics of Children

In the *middle* stage of childhood (approximately ages six to eight), children have vivid imaginations and are usually curious and eager to learn.

As they grow physically, children develop a heightened sense of sexual differentiation. At this time, they need to be reassured of their specialness and goodness in being a boy or a girl.

Peer relationships become increasingly important, while the family maintains its significance. Through these relationships, children develop appropriate social skills as well as the qualities required in being a friend to others.

While children in this stage have a tendency to be self-centered, they are able to cooperate and assume responsibility. Rules and guidelines begin to influence their behavior.

Spiritually, children are attracted to images of Jesus, stories from Scripture, and opportunities for prayer and ritual celebration.

In the *later* stage of childhood (usually ages nine to eleven), children are in a period of relative physical stability. They are either growing at a steady rate or in small spurts. Some children will experience the onset of puberty, the dawn of adolescence, earlier than others. As a consequence, there is a growing evidence of self-consciousness about the body, preoccupation with secondary sexual characteristics, and a heightened sense of competition related to physical growth and appearance.

Peer group relationships and values become more important as does the need for acceptance. Socially, there is a tendency toward seeking friends of the same sex, while some boys and girls will begin to develop relationships with the other sex.

At this time in their lives, children develop cognitive abilities and begin processing abstract ideas and values. They are able to discuss issues, analyze situations, and draw conclusions. Children possess an increased capacity to appreciate the need for rules so as to ensure an orderliness in their lives and relationships. Developing a greater awareness of what is morally right and of their own strengths and limitations, children learn to make reasonable choices. They also grow in an awareness and concern for other persons.

Spiritually, children grow in their knowledge and understanding of God, Church, sacraments, Scripture, Christian living, and of themselves as unique persons created by God. Prayer and celebration continue to be a major focus of their religious expression.

Guidelines for Childhood

The following guidelines apply when educating children about human sexuality. They are to be used in conjunction with Human Sexuality: A Catholic Perspective for Education and Lifelong Learning *and with the* General Principles *that are included in this Appendix. These* General Principles *apply to all stages of development. It is helpful to remember that one stage builds on another, and that stages of growth and development often overlap.*

Because children at this age can experience the life-enriching qualities of belonging to a loving Christian community of family and church, educators in human sexuality need to support and create environments in which children can grow. Some areas to address include:

- providing opportunities for families to learn, pray, and socialize;

- helping children and adults recognize how love creates life and helps it to grow;

- affirming human relationships that are faithful and trusting, especially those of parents and family members; and

- inviting adults who are good role models to share their time and gifts with children.

Because children at this age are still greatly influenced by their parents and families, educators need to affirm parents as the primary educators of their children. Some areas to address include:

- involving parents in planning and evaluating programs in human sexuality;

- providing opportunities for parents to learn how to communicate effectively with their children; and

- creating intergenerational experiences and materials.

Because children at this age are beginning to ask about and understand their own growth in sexuality, educators need to provide opportunities for children to learn about and respond to these changes. Some areas to address include:

- teaching children about their developing bodies and helping them to understand basic physiological processes;

- helping children develop habits of caring for the body; and

- assisting children to understand the importance of modesty, self-discipline, and the need for privacy.

Because children at this age are conscious of growing friendships in their lives, educators need to help parents/guardians affirm children as they experience new feelings and encourage them to appreciate and learn how to deal with these feelings. Some areas to address include:

- helping children relate to persons of the same and the other sex;

- teaching skills of honest communication, listening, sharing, forgiving, trusting;

- affirming the equality of men and women in word, attitude, and action; and

- helping children become conscious of barriers in relationships, such as cultural stereotyping.

Because children at this age have an increasing understanding of what is right and wrong, educators need to help children to recognize that some behavior is harmful and unacceptable to growth in relationships, and to realize their own goodness as God intends them to be. Some areas to address include:

- assisting children to recognize that they are both loved and able to love;

- enabling children to reflect on their experiences of love by family and friends;

- helping children identify genuine and appropriate expressions of love;

- instructing children how to express love for others in a genuine and appropriate way;

- teaching children how to accept and love others who are different from them; and

- enabling children to celebrate forgiveness in the sacrament of reconciliation and everyday life.

Because children at this age have a growing sense of God and Church, educators need to help children integrate their beliefs and values into their ongoing education in human sexuality. Some areas to address include:

- connecting family faith life and more formal instruction;

- teaching prayer based on life experience;

- helping children understand their growing relationship with God;

- preparing children for Eucharist and reconciliation; and

- familiarizing children with Scripture and how it applies to their lives.

Because children at this age are influenced by television, videos, and other media, educators need to help parents/guardians know how to talk with their children about the values and attitudes that media portrays. Some areas to address include:

- sexist attitudes;

- portrayal of sex as a commodity;

- sexually transmitted diseases (STDs);

- child and sexual abuse;

- sexual orientation;

- role models;

- family models; and

- experiences of brokenness, separation, death, loss.

For further development of the issues identified in these guidelines, refer to the text of the foundational document.

Early Adolescence

This developmental stage builds on childhood. Some of the characteristics will overlap, as will some of the guidelines. Youth in this stage of development will possess varying degrees of maturity and of readiness for education in human sexuality. Educators need to make adaptations accordingly.

Characteristics of Early Adolescents

The early adolescent developmental stage usually occurs during or just before the earliest teenage years. Physical and emotional changes and growth are accelerated.

Usually, young adolescents experience the initiation of rapid physical growth while their psychological and emotional growth is well on the way. During this period of physical growth, it is likely that early adolescents feel awkward, confused, and uneasy about their bodies.

At this time in their lives, early adolescents become intensely concerned about their self-identity and are interested in learning more about themselves, which leads them through a period of self-consciousness.

Early adolescents tend to initiate their move toward independence. They seek out others like themselves and move beyond the family circle. Concern for self and peer relationships are both quite important at this stage, so they find themselves most comfortable with others of their own age and sex, but gain more confidence and comfort in mixed groups.

Thoughts and feelings about their own human sexuality become prominent in the life of early adolescents. This heightened awareness of their sexual attributes normally causes increased anxiety, confusion, and fear about these personal developments.

In the area of decision making, early adolescents often may question traditional rules and struggle to make personal decisions even though they lack the experiences that would help them anticipate the possible consequences of their decisions.

At this stage of their spiritual development, early adolescents seek a more personal relationship with God. This relationship is often nourished by the faith of the family and the sacraments of the Church. Involvement of young adolescents in the life or formal religious activities of the Church depends to a large measure on parental encouragement and support as well as peer participation.

They tend to become active participants in church life and ministry if their parents are involved and if encouraged by personal or peer group invitation.

Guidelines for Early Adolescence

The following guidelines apply when educating early adolescents about human sexuality. They are to be used in conjunction with Human Sexuality: A Catholic Perspective for Education and Lifelong Learning *and with the* General Principles *that are included in this Appendix. These* General Principles *apply to all stages of development. It is helpful to remember that one stage builds on another, and that stages of growth and development often overlap.*

Because early adolescents at this stage may differ in their maturity level in many areas, it is important for educators to be sensitive to the need to adapt instructional material, methods, and consideration of times when same sex or individual instruction is more appropriate. Some areas to address include:

- teaching early adolescents respect for their bodies;

- explaining to early adolescents the nature of personal maturation;

- helping early adolescents to deal with their own growth, maturation, and the consequent psychological effects; and

- reaffirming for early adolescents the value of personal modesty.

Because early adolescence presents youth with many new experiences, both physical and emotional, educators need to work with parents, families, and early adolescents to assist them in making sense of these new experiences (e.g., menstruation and nocturnal emissions) in ways that respect the early adolescence experience and that honor the dignity of sexuality from a Catholic perspective. Some areas to address include:

- reassuring early adolescents that sexual attraction is natural and normal;

- instructing early adolescents on proper hygiene and health care for their developing bodies;

- assisting early adolescents to develop good nutritional habits and regular exercise routines;

- informing early adolescents of the health hazard that smoking presents; and

- educating early adolescents on the deleterious effects of alcohol and drug abuse on physical and mental health.

Because physical growth is such a dominant concern at this stage, it is especially important for educators to teach the purpose, respect, and care of the body, encouraging parents/guardians to do the same. Some areas to address include:

- providing early adolescents with an understanding of the biological processes of the body appropriate to their stage of development;

- teaching early adolescents the basic facts of human fertility and reproduction in the context of Christian marriage; and

- extolling the virtue of chastity and the right of early adolescents to bodily integrity, including respect for and from others.

Because early adolescents are becoming more aware of the power of their own sexuality, educators need to help them understand that the human person is called to experience and express love by means of the body in appropriate and respectful ways. Some areas to address include:

- reassuring early adolescents that they have the capacity both to love and to be loved;

- assisting early adolescents to recognize the role and model of parents and family regarding love and relationships;

- instructing early adolescents in the appropriate ways of expressing love physically and emotionally; and

- teaching early adolescents that Christian marriage is the context in which love is expressed fully by means of the body.

Because early adolescents look for guides and adult models, it is necessary for educators to tell the story of Jesus and other holy people, models who show us how to appreciate, make decisions about, and live out this gift of sexuality. Some areas to address include:

- encouraging early adolescents to become familiar with the

life and story of Jesus as the model for personal maturity, friendships, and relational skills;

- making available to early adolescents the lives of the saints for inspiration and as models for imitation; and

- identifying and fostering adult role models and mentors in the family, school, church, and local community.

Because the gifts of sexuality and sex can be abused, it is timely for educators to help parents/guardians to reaffirm that some touches are inappropriate and may be sexual abuse, and to give guidance on how to resist the temptations of immoral, aberrant, and inappropriate sexual behavior. Some areas to address include:

- teaching early adolescents how to deal morally with pornographic literature, abusive language, and the exploitation of sex and sexuality in movies, television, music, videos, and other forms of entertainment;

- informing early adolescents about the Church's teaching and pastoral approaches to the issue of masturbation;

- instructing early adolescents on the Church's tradition regarding genital sex outside of marriage;

- informing early adolescents of the nature and effects of sexually transmitted diseases; and

- providing a simple explanation of church teaching regarding heterosexuality and homosexuality.

Because early adolescents may begin to explore, experiment, and experience their sexuality in new ways, educators need to explain Catholic moral principles involved and teach them the moral decision-making process. Some areas to address include:

- teaching early adolescents the art of moral decision making, moving from values to general norms to application in specific moral situations;

- providing early adolescents and their families with the necessary resources (e.g., Scripture, church teachings, prudent counsel) for the formation of a good conscience;

- assisting early adolescents in developing a sense of personal and social responsibility concerning the consequences of their choices and actions;

- preparing early adolescents and their parents/guardians for the reception of the sacraments; and

- encouraging early adolescents to receive the sacraments of reconciliation and the Eucharist regularly.

For further development of the issues identified in these guidelines, refer to the text of the foundational document.

Adolescence

This developmental stage builds on early adolescence. Some of the characteristics will overlap, as will some of the guidelines. Since youth in this stage of development will express many levels of maturity, educators need to make adaptations accordingly.

Characteristics of Adolescents

Adolescence is a time of intense physical, emotional, intellectual, social, and spiritual growth. The rapid physical changes include growth in height, weight, muscle, and sexual characteristics. These changes have a profound effect on the emotional, psychological, and relational development of adolescents. During this stage, youth discover themselves primarily through their interpersonal relationships. What was once a self-centeredness in childhood begins to give way to concern for others.

Issues such as the quality of male and female relationships, the peer and adult models that impress adolescents, and the variety of human experience that surrounds adolescents take on new significance. This step in growth is fluid, and, therefore, the adolescent experience is not always a step-by-step movement. Personal choice becomes even more of a reality due to increased independence, expanding personal freedom, and a desire for autonomy. New experiences such as dating, infatuation, physical affection, sexual orientation, parental limits, and church guidelines all challenge adolescents to find answers for new questions. The adolescent experience is a growing awareness that important choices are being made daily.

Adolescents, too, are becoming more capable of abstract thought, challenging argumentation, and private spirituality. Searching for an authentic spirituality, adolescents are increasingly aware of their inner life and are becoming aware of universal moral principles. In short, adolescents are building the necessary components of their future adult life. As such, their thinking, choices, and actions about sex and sexuality become a more complex process. Added to this is their increased awareness of fairness, justice, and equality. They are awakening to the transcendent.

Guidelines for Adolescence

The following guidelines apply when educating adolescents about human sexuality. They are to be used in conjunction with Human Sexuality: A

Catholic Perspective for Education and Lifelong Learning and with the General Principles *that are included in this Appendix. These* General Principles *apply to all stages of development. It is helpful to remember that one stage builds on another, and that stages of growth and development often overlap.*

Because this may be the last opportunity for adolescents to receive formal education in sexuality, educators need to help parents/guardians to provide positive instruction about the wonder of the human body, sexual functioning, fertility, and reproduction, and how to appreciate and care for their bodies in life-giving ways. Some areas to address include:

- providing adolescents with the biological facts about human sexuality and reproductive processes of the body;

- instructing adolescents in the unitive and procreative purposes of marriage and sexual activity therein;

- teaching adolescents respect for their own bodies and those of others;

- encouraging adolescents to develop positive hygienic practices;

- assisting adolescents in developing good nutritional habits and regular exercise routines; and

- informing adolescents of the harmful effects of smoking, alcohol, and other chemical substances on the body.

Because love and sex are often equated, educators and parents/guardians need to explain the full meaning of love in the context of the gospels. Some areas to address include:

- providing adolescents with a thorough explanation of the nature of love; and

- distinguishing for adolescents the meaning of sexuality and sex from the Catholic perspective.

Because Jesus showed everyone how to be fully human and how to develop friendships, educators and parents/guardians need to proclaim the story of Jesus. Some areas to address include:

- encouraging adolescents to adopt Jesus as the model for personal maturity and committed friendship;

- recommending that adolescents find models and mentors, mature and prudent persons in whom they can confide;

- providing adolescents with skills to assist them in developing healthy friendships; and

- instructing adolescents on the mutual responsibilities of friendship.

Because human beings sin—fail to love God, their neighbor, and themselves—they are in need of forgiveness and reconciliation. Therefore, educators and parents/guardians need to proclaim and model God's readiness to forgive, and encourage adolescents to reconciliation. Some areas to address include:

- instructing adolescents on the nature and effects of sin, including those related to sexuality, affecting one's own psychosexual development as well as impacting one's relationships with others;

- teaching adolescents about God's forgiveness as expressed by Jesus in his life and ministry; and

- encouraging adolescents to celebrate regularly the sacraments of Eucharist and reconciliation.

Because normal impulses and feelings of adolescents lead them toward sexual experimentation and expressions, educators need to assist parents/guardians in explaining the Church's position on sexual intimacy. They need to reaffirm the value of personal modesty, the avoidance of sexually suggestive situations and entertainment, and to lend their support to adolescents making healthy and moral choices. Some areas to address include:

- promoting among adolescents the values of modesty and chastity;

- instructing adolescents on the appropriate expressions of love for their state of life;

- fostering in adolescents a wholesome respect for the equality and mutuality of the sexes;

- teaching adolescents that genital sexual intimacy finds its proper place only in the context of marriage;

- helping adolescents to develop as healthy and mature sexual persons, capable of responsible relationships, avoiding occasions of sexual immorality; and

- instructing adolescents on a moral decision-making process rooted in gospel values and church teaching.

Because adolescents are approaching an age when they may take on the permanent commitment of marriage, educators need to provide information and instruction on marriage from the Catholic perspective. Some areas to address include:

- teaching and modeling for adolescents wholesome personal relationships with the same and opposite sex;

- providing a course of instruction for adolescents on engagement, marriage, and parenting from a Catholic perspective; and

- informing adolescents of the Church's teaching and pastoral approaches regarding divorce, annulment, and remarriage.

Because the Church provides guidance to adolescents about objective right and wrong and is an integral resource in their conscience formation, educators need to inform adolescents and their families about the Church's teachings on contemporary moral issues. Some areas to address include:

- instructing adolescents on the Church's teachings concerning masturbation, nonmarital sex, and contraception;

- teaching adolescents how to deal morally with pornography and the exploitation of sex and sexuality in entertainment;

- providing adolescents with a simple explanation of the Church's teachings regarding reproductive technology and sterilization;

- teaching adolescents about heterosexuality and homosexuality from a Catholic perspective;

- informing adolescents of their right to bodily integrity and the need for that to be respected by oneself and others; and

- instructing adolescents on the source, nature, and effects of sexually transmitted diseases.

For further development of the issues identified in these guidelines, refer to the text of the foundational document.

Adulthood

This developmental stage builds on adolescence. Unlike other phases, there are several stages in adulthood, not solely dependent on chronological age. These developmental stages, which are quite varied throughout the adult life-span, can be grouped basically into young, middle, and older adulthood. Maturity levels will vary within age groupings, backgrounds, and life experience. Educators need to know their audience and make adaptations accordingly.

Characteristics of Adults

Young adulthood is a life passage filled with many changes and transitions. Career changes, emotional changes, physical changes, and psychological changes make up the life of the young adult. This time of passage from adolescence to middle adulthood is a time in the life of a person when choices are verified and experimentation is often a part of coming to full maturation.

Many young adults are in the "searching faith" stage of development. They are seeking a faith that they can live by, one that is their own. Consequently, young adults question the values, beliefs, and traditions of their parents. Critical during this time are mentors and "mentoring" communities, who model the values and traditions that the young adult is searching for and attempting to clarify. They foster in the young adult the establishment of an "own faith," providing them with tools that will carry them through the next stage of life.

As people move toward middle adulthood, they have a clearer sense of their identity, sexual orientation, competencies, and limitations. They bring to learning rich life experiences that serve as a resource to other people. Their continued growth as adults is dependent upon their drawing meaning out of their life experiences. Middle adults often have attained independence and self-direction and developed a value system, but they continue to struggle with social pressures and peer approval. Most middle adults have learned to be friends and colleagues and may maintain long-standing, deeply shared relationships. They know appropriate ways of relating to other people in various settings.

As adults move through life, especially as they enter their "senior" years, they become increasingly concerned with the differences their lives will make in the order of things. They want to know and feel that their lives have been valuable. Those who have more fully matured during adulthood care especially about passing along to the next generation those things that have most enriched their lives, such as faith, values, truths, customs, organizations, and institutions.

Ironically, at the same time that older adults are growing "in age, grace, and wisdom," they must face the inevitable frustrations of the aging process. Retirement from a lifetime career brings with it both loss and leisure. Older adults frequently face some degree of declining health as well as the loss through death of spouses, family members, and beloved friends. However, their sexuality needs—to love and to be loved, to touch and to be touched—remain throughout life. Social, educational, and spiritual opportunities, focused on the special needs of older adults, are essential if we are to foster lifelong learning.

Adults at every stage examine and make choices about life-style patterns as single persons, married persons, or vowed celibates. Each life-style presents the adult with its own challenges and opportunities.

Finally, adults seek an integrated and meaningful spirituality that helps them cope with life's challenges and establish a satisfying relationship with God.

Guidelines for Adulthood

The following guidelines apply when educating adults about human sexuality. They are to be used in conjunction with Human Sexuality: A Catholic Perspective for Education and Lifelong Learning *and with the* General Principles *that are included in this Appendix. These* General Principles *apply to all stages of development. It is helpful to remember that one stage builds on another, and that stages of growth and development often overlap.*

Because the sources of sexual information and formation are numerous, varied, conflicting, and sometimes so subtle as to be virtually unnoticed, educators need to develop, support, and encourage ongoing education for adults. Some areas to address include:

- providing knowledge of changing relationships in the developmental stages of adulthood;

- providing opportunities for developing good communication skills, which are essential for healthy relationships;

- exploring life-style choices (single, married, vowed religious) in light of fidelity to chastity, commitment, and growth in intimacy with persons of the same and opposite sex;

- assisting adults in using their reasoning ability, the sources of divine revelation, the Church's teaching and guidance, the wise counsel of others, and their own individual and communal experience of grace to make good moral decisions;

- providing times for and methods of reflection, prayer, and discussion as well as sacramental opportunities;

- fostering Christian community-building and worship experiences;

- fostering an appreciation for ongoing knowledge about moral issues involved in reproduction, such as sterilization, new developments in reproductive technology, spacing of children (NFP), and contraception;

- fostering in parents an awareness of their familial responsibilities, including the privilege and duty of providing a Christian family environment, in which a positive and moral understanding of human sexuality is modeled, taught, and encouraged;

- providing educational opportunities to parents and guardians to enhance both their parenting skills and their ability to contribute wisely and well to the sexuality education of children entrusted to them; in this context, parents themselves may very well serve as ministers to other parents and to guardians;

- helping adults to be informed about sexual dysfunction, sexual abuse, and sexually transmitted diseases; and

- offering to adults at every stage of development the information and formational opportunities necessary to live faithfully and responsibly the physical, psychological, social, and spiritual dimensions of life.

For further development of the issues identified in these guidelines, refer to the text of the foundational document.

Conclusion

We encourage you to continue your ministry as a leader in education in human sexuality. Your task is not easy. Lifelong learning requires commitment to a process that unfolds and deepens through the years. Your ministry calls for listening, sensitivity, and a passion for the truth. We ask you to continue to grow through prayer, reflection, study, and dialogue as you journey with those you serve. Know that we are with you in that ongoing process of discovery.

Bibliography of Church Documents Related to Education in Human Sexuality

Conciliar Decrees

Vatican Council II. *Declaration on Christian Education.* October 28, 1965.

_____. *Declaration on Religious Freedom.* December 7, 1965.

_____. *Decree on the Apostolate of the Laity.* November 18, 1965. Esp. nos. 11-14.

_____. *Decree on the Appropriate Renewal of the Religious Life.* October 28, 1965.

_____. *Decree on the Instruments of Social Communication.* December 4, 1963.

_____. *Decree on the Ministry and Life of Priests.* December 7, 1965.

_____. *Pastoral Constitution on the Church in the Modern World.* December 7, 1965. Esp. nos. 16, 47-52.

Papal Documents

John Paul II. *Code of Canon Law (Codex Iuris Canonici).* Revised 1983. Esp. Title VII: Marriage, cc. 1055-1165. [This 1983 revision of the 1917 *Code,* while promulgated by John Paul II, is obviously the work of a much broader group of ecclesial personnel.]

_____. *On the Dignity and Vocation of Women (Mulieris Dignitatem).* Apostolic Letter. August 15, 1988.

_____. *On the Family (Familiaris Consortio)*. Apostolic Exhortation. December 15, 1981.

_____. *On the Vocation and Mission of the Lay Faithful in the World (Christifideles Laici)*. Apostolic Exhortation. December 30, 1988.

_____. *To the Youth of the World*. Apostolic Letter. March 31, 1985.

Paul VI. *On the Regulation of Birth (Humanae Vitae)*. Encyclical Letter. July 25, 1968.

Pius XI. *On Christian Marriage (Casti Connubii)*. Encyclical Letter. December 31, 1930.

Pius XII. *Address to Italian Midwives*. October 29, 1951.

> [In addition to these "official" papal decrees, John Paul II has made the topic of sexuality the focus of a number of his general audiences and conferences.]

John Paul II. *Blessed Are the Pure of Heart: Catechesis on the Sermon on the Mount and the Writings of St. Paul*. Boston: Daughters of St. Paul, 1983.

_____. *Original Unity of Man and Woman: Catechesis on the Book of Genesis*. September 5, 1979 to April 2, 1980. Boston: Daughters of St. Paul, 1981.

_____. *Reflections on "Humanae Vitae": Conjugal Morality and Spirituality*. Boston: Daughters of St. Paul, 1984.

Documents from Vatican Offices or Congregations

Congregation for Catholic Education. *Educational Guidance in Human Love*. November 1, 1983.

_____. *The Religious Dimension of Education in a Catholic School*. April 7, 1988.

Congregation for the Doctrine of the Faith. *Declaration on Certain Questions Concerning Sexual Ethics*. December 29, 1975.

_____. *Instruction on Respect for Life in Its Origin and on the*

Dignity of Procreation: Replies to Certain Questions of the Day.
February 22, 1987.

_____. *Letter to the Bishops of the Catholic Church on the Pastoral Care of Homosexual Persons.* October 1, 1986.

Holy See. *Charter of the Rights of the Family.* October 22, 1983.

The International Theological Commission. *Faith and Inculturation.* October 1988.

Pontifical Council of Social Communication. *Pornography and Violence in the Media: A Pastoral Response.* May 7, 1989.

Documents Approved by the NCCB/USCC

National Conference of Catholic Bishops. *Called to Compassion and Responsibility: A Response to the HIV/AIDS Crisis.* November 1989. Washington, D.C.: USCC Office for Publishing and Promotion Services, 1989.

_____. *Human Life in Our Day.* A Pastoral Letter. November 15, 1968. Washington, D.C.: USCC Office for Publishing and Promotion Services, 1968.

_____. *Sharing the Light of Faith: National Catechetical Directory for Catholics of the United States.* Washington, D.C.: USCC Office for Publishing and Promotion Services, 1979. With the Approval of the Sacred Congregation for the Clergy.

_____. *Sharing the Light of Faith: An Official Commentary.* Washington, D.C.: USCC Office for Publishing and Promotion Services, 1981.

_____. *Statement on School-based Clinics.* November 18, 1987. Washington, D.C.: USCC Office for Publishing and Promotion Services, 1987.

_____. *To Live in Christ Jesus: A Pastoral Reflection on the Moral Life.* November 11, 1976. Washington, D.C.: USCC Office for Publishing and Promotion Services, 1976.

_____. *To Teach as Jesus Did: A Pastoral Message on Catholic Education.* November 1972. Washington, D.C.: USCC Office for Publishing and Promotion Services, 1972.

Documents from NCCB/USCC Committees or Departments

Ad Hoc Committee on Marriage and Family Life, NCCB. *A Family Perspective in Church and Society: A Manual for All Pastoral Leaders*. Washington, D.C.: USCC Office for Publishing and Promotion Services, 1988.

Administrative Board, USCC. *The Many Faces of AIDS: A Gospel Response*. November 1987. Washington, D.C.: USCC Office for Publishing and Promotion Services, 1987.

Bishops' Committee for Pastoral Research and Practices, NCCB. *Faithful to Each Other Forever: A Catholic Handbook of Pastoral Help for Marriage Preparation*. Washington, D.C.: USCC Office for Publishing and Promotion Services, 1989.

_____. *Principles to Guide Confessors in Questions of Homosexuality*. Washington, D.C.: USCC Office for Publishing and Promotion Services, 1973.

Bishops' Committee on Priestly Life and Ministry, NCCB. *A Reflection on Human Sexuality and the Ordained Priesthood*. Washington, D.C.: USCC Office for Publishing and Promotion Services, 1983. Authorized by the entire NCCB (November, 1978). Reviewed by Administrative Committee (September, 1982). Approved for Publication by Bishop Justin A. Driscoll, Chair (November 10, 1982).

Department of Education, USCC. *The Single Experience: A Resource*. Reflections and Models for Single Young Adulthood. Washington, D.C.: USCC Office for Publishing and Promotion Services, 1979.

National Committee on Human Sexuality Education/Department of Education, USCC. *Education in Human Sexuality for Christians*. Washington, D.C.: USCC Office for Publishing and Promotion Services, 1981.

United States Catholic Conference. *Pastoral Statement of U.S. Catholic Bishops on Persons with Disabilities*. November 16, 1978. Revised 1989. Washington, D.C.: USCC Office for Publishing and Promotion Services, 1978/1989.

Documents by Local Bishops or by State Bishops' Conferences

Bernadin, Cardinal Joseph. *Sexuality and Church Teaching.* September 29, 1980. Remarks at International Synod on the Family in Rome.

_____. *Statement on the Evening Mass at St. Sebastian and Ministry to Homosexuals.* May 15, 1988. Reprinted in *Origins* 17 (June 9, 1988): 49, 51.

Bishops of the Dioceses of New Jersey. *A Joint Pastoral Statement on Education in Human Sexuality.* December 9, 1980.

California Catholic Conference. *Principles and Guidelines for the Development of Public Policy Regarding AIDS/ARC.* January 14, 1988. Reprinted in *Origins* 17 (January 28, 1988): 561, 563-565.

Connecticut Catholic Conference. *After the Sexual Revolution.* February 17, 1989.

_____. *Statement of the Catholic Bishops of Connecticut on Sex Education in Public Schools.* Spring 1980. Available through the Office of Radio and TV, Hartford, Connecticut.

Massachusetts Catholic Conference. *Sex Education: Information or Formation?* November 20, 1987. Reprinted in *Origins* 17 (December 31, 1987): 510-511.

Mugavero, Bishop Francis J. *Sexuality—God's Gift: A Pastoral Letter.* February 11, 1976. Reprinted in *Catholic Mind* (May 1976): 53-58.

Pennsylvania Catholic Conference. *To Love and to Be Loved: The Pennsylvania Bishops Speak to Youth on the Gift of Sexuality.* January 1989.

Roach, Archbishop John R. *Grateful for the Gift: Sexuality, Parents and Teens.* A Letter to Parents. March 1988. Reprinted in *Origins* 17 (March 17, 1988): 690-692.

Texas Catholic Conference. *Texas Bishops' Statement on Sexuality.* January 4, 1988. Reprinted in *Origins* 17 (January 14, 1988): 541-544.